Brenda V. Ackroyd

A Foretaste of Heaven

Stories inspired by the Mysteries of the Rosary

Don Bosco
Publications

Don Bosco Publications
Thornleigh House, Sharples Park, Bolton BL1 6PQ
United Kingdom

ISBN 978-1-909080-78-2
©Don Bosco Publications 2021
©Brenda Ackroyd

The moral rights of the author have been asserted

Front cover photo by Patrick Pahlke on Unsplash

Printed in Malta by Melita Press

A Prayer

Oh God, whose only begotten Son, by his Life, Death and Resurrection, has purchased for us the rewards of eternal life, grant we beseech thee that, by meditating on these mysteries of the most Holy Rosary of the Blessed Virgin Mary, we may both imitate what they contain and obtain what they promise, through the same Christ, Our Lord.

Amen.

Contents

Introduction

I have no theological qualifications or expertise to justify my writing a book on a religious topic. Nor was this book preconceived as a complete work of reflection on the Mysteries of the Holy Rosary. I do have faith, however, and I trust in the Lord and in his Blessed Mother, Mary. From small and simple beginnings, this little book just grew.

I belonged to a local group, based in East Cheshire, of the ecumenical Association of Christian Writers. Between meetings, we completed pieces of homework, and one of these was to rewrite a Bible story from the point of view of one of the participants. From one homework piece, I went on to write one or two others. It proved a really good way to become immersed in scriptural events, to explore the characters involved and reflect on their qualities and experience. It was a sort of written extension of *Lectio Divina*, I suppose. I often found it deeply moving.

Writing has always been an interest of mine. I am a retired teacher of English Language and Literature, and so was well used to a literary fiction style. Stories in the scriptures are told so succinctly, that they seemed to me to cry out for expansion. They can be so short that we may pass them by without realising the scope of their significance. Of course, lengthy treatment would have been an impossible luxury at the time when they were first recorded because they had to be handwritten on perhaps limited or expensive supplies of parchment or vellum, then copied laboriously by scribes each time a further copy was required. Perhaps, in consequence, people then valued the written word so highly that they lingered over every phrase. Nowadays we are used to reading much more quickly, sometimes just scanning a newspaper, for instance, because there really isn't time in the day to read it all. This is a different age. So, I wrote my stories.

It wasn't long before I realised that most of them were about the events which were also the great Mysteries of the Holy Rosary. Since Saint Pope John Paul II added the five Luminous Mysteries in 2002, there have been twenty Mysteries in total. Why not see if I could write stories for them all? I had occasionally thought of writing something in appreciation of the Rosary Mysteries, maybe a poem for each one. Stories provided a much more promising, expansive canvas.

If you can think of all the teachings and stories in the New Testament as a sort of box of treasures, then to me the Rosary Mysteries are the greatest jewels among them. It is no wonder the Church's tradition encourages us to meditate upon them as we recite the Hail Marys and other prayers of the Rosary. Like precious jewels, they reward our gazing into the depth of their colours and wondering at their many-faceted lights and aspects.

Some of the Mysteries, as I progressed, posed difficult problems. The Last Glorious Mysteries, for instance, concerning Mary's Assumption and her Coronation as the Queen of Heaven, lay somewhat beyond the scope of my experience—or the experience of any of us, come to that, because we have not yet lived beyond the bounds of this world! But by now I had a real conviction that I was meant to finish the task. I ventured on these problematic stories with a huge amount of prayer! I am convinced Our Lady came to my help. Some of the problems are referred to in the course of the introductory commentaries before each story, which, incidentally, were not pre-planned either.

When complete, I showed the stories to a number of friends. One of these, whom I am privileged to know, Father Martin Onuoha, currently serving as a parish priest in Stockport, suggested that they might be augmented by reflections and prayers. It was a really helpful idea, because it enabled me to go a step further, relating the stories' events, characters and implications to our own lives—to readers' lives—in the world today.

Of course, I do not claim that my stories contain all the significance of the biblical or traditional events they portray; not by a very long chalk! There could be countless other versions, picking up on other characters, aspects and values. This is part of the joy of the Mysteries. Their fruits are infinite.

My hope for this book is that these expanded versions of the stories of major events in the lives of Jesus and his Mother will draw readers into their depths as much as they drew me. I hope they will enable readers to linger longer within and explore more fully all the interplay of the human and the divine which lies at their heart. I hope that this experience will lead readers into meditating on the full significance of the events within the stories and into considering how they should influence our prayers, our choices and the direction of our lives.

I would like to place on record my thanks to Father Martin Onuoha for his invaluable suggestion and support, and also to Mrs Gillian Henn, who led the East Cheshire Group affiliated to the Association of Christian Writers, and who, in addition to providing lots of encouragement, proposed the homework which got me started. I am extremely grateful also to Father Bob Gardner and Ms Sarah Seddon of Don Bosco Publications, for all their help and advice in bringing this book to publication. It seems to me that we have all been "links in a chain", to use St John Henry Newman's wonderful phrase, and I am endlessly grateful to God, who, I feel sure, was the guiding hand behind it all. Praise and Glory to Him!

The Joyful Mysteries

1. The Annunciation

This, the first Joyful Mystery, is where it all begins. This is where God's plan for our salvation first breaks into human experience on Earth. This is where we witness the young Virgin Mary's amazing "yes" to the angel's message that she is to bear God's own Son, thus allowing God's plan to come to fruition. Mary wonders at God's plan but agrees to it without hesitation—and she agrees once and for all. She never deviates from that decision despite its inevitable and considerable costs.

One of the first of these costs is the effect of her decision on her betrothed, Joseph. How must it all have seemed to him? Perhaps his experience was something like the following story.

Mary is With Child

How I long to reach her! Thoughts teem in my mind, realisations, changes I am desperate to explain. I was so wrong—and now the only thing that matters is to set things right. I want to fly to her, to soar over obstacles like a bird. But as I labour up the narrow street of Nazareth, avoiding insistent street vendors on the way, I feel more like a beetle struggling through a field of brittle hay stalks than a bird in flight. I burn with impatience.

It isn't just the physical obstacles in my way that I have to contend with; it is people's expectations, traditions, normality. Walking here, making my way to the home of my intended future wife, I am breaking every rule in the book. Had you told me, even just a week ago, that I would be doing this, I wouldn't have believed you.

Here in Galilee, as in Judaea as well, a bridegroom does not visit his betrothed before the two come to be united in matrimony. If there is some vital message to be conveyed, it is the role of the groom's best friend to undertake it. Which is why I had to despatch Reuben two weeks ago. He carried my terrible decision to Mary. It was cruel; I can see that now. But at the time I felt I had no choice. I had had incredible news delivered to me.

"Mary is with child." I will never forget the way Reuben reluctantly pronounced those words, his eyes deliberately avoiding mine. I protested. I told him it was nonsense. It just couldn't possibly be true. Reuben only shook his head and apologised. He passed on some rumoured story about an angel having visited her. It only made it worse, colouring Mary with ridicule as well as disgrace. As if one of God's angels could bring such a thing to pass!

My disbelief was rapidly pursued by horror at the prospect of the consequences which must surely ensue. Grief, shock and consternation battled in my heart. I could not bear—even if her betrayal of me proved real—I could not bear to think how she would suffer.

It gave me a small measure of relief when Reuben advised me that a private and informal divorce would spare her some of the public humiliation and shame. So, this was the decision with which I sent Reuben on his way to Nazareth. He assured me that I had chosen the kindest course, and I assured myself that I was only acting for the best. But I was sick at heart. The light of joy that Mary had kindled in my life was utterly extinguished.

That was until last night, when it happened. A startling dream. I seemed to be wandering in a desert landscape, when a tall, white-clad figure appeared from nowhere in front of me. He looked right into my eyes from his own copper-coloured, beautiful eyes, and I knew he was from heaven.

"Joseph," his voice was very calm and gentle. "Joseph, do not be afraid to take Mary as your wife." The words penetrated right to my heart and allayed all the pain of loss and desolation that lay there. A huge peace filled me. I stood motionless.

"She has conceived what is in her by the Holy Spirit," the angel went on to explain. There was such grace in his tone. Then it strengthened as he declared, "She will give birth to a son and you must name him Jesus, because he is the one who is to save his people from their sins."

I held my breath in awe. Mary—blessed by such a gift from God? Was she to give birth to our Messiah? Mary—but she was a child! Then it jumped into my mind: the memory of how God had chosen my ancestor David—the youngest of Jesse's family, a child—to be our future king. It had to be true. I had made a huge mistake. I turned away from the caring face of the angel, needing a few moments to face this new truth: that I had misjudged her so callously. I had hurt her—I must have damaged her deeply. By the time I looked back at my visitor to confess this, he had vanished from sight. I was too overcome to move from that spot in the desert. I sank onto a gently rising hillock in the sand and remained there, holding his words to myself.

When the light of morning woke me, the dream rushed back and took possession of me. It was a message from God. There was not one iota of doubt in me. Despite the immensity of the message, in seconds my mind vaulted all the difficulties and complexities I had been mired in. I saw it clear as day. Mary had been gifted by God with a child. Not just a child, but a child of God! And I, in my utterly clumsy humanity, had sought to protect my own pathetic reputation by a separation from her.

Dear God, how I must have made her suffer! She must be feeling utterly alone and terrified. My precious girl—the woman I would wed now, whatever other people thought. I wasted no time in dressing, setting my business to rights and leaving on a journey into Nazareth.

Now I near the house at last. I do not hesitate. I stride to the door and knock vigorously on it. I expect it to be her mother who responds to this imperious summons, but when the door opens just a little, I behold the face of Mary gazing from troubled eyes, with an expression of nervousness which I have not seen there before.

"Mary!" I exclaim. She simply stares. "Mary, I need to come in. I need to explain. I need you to forgive me." The words tumble from me uncontrollably. "I'm so sorry for the message Reuben brought."

The large eyes blink and continue to stare at me for what seems like hours. She knows, as I do, that this meeting is totally improper. I am reduced to silence. Finally, she draws the door more fully open and allows me to step inside. "Thank you. I'm so sorry, Mary. Mary, I was wrong." I stammer there in the doorway like a boy.

She goes ahead, leading me into the house. I follow.

When she reaches the hearth and the benches round it, she turns to face me. Her eyes are downcast, but I see that the lids are red from weeping. My heart aches to protect her. How do I explain?

"I had a visit from an angel," I state abruptly. "He changed everything."

Her eyes lift to my face with a new curiosity. "An angel?" she says. "Truly? Did you see him?"

"In a dream," I answer, "but he must have been a messenger from God. Beautiful eyes. And a voice I could not doubt."

She turns away, gazing into a distance. I wonder if I have left it all too late.

"He was huge, my angel," she murmurs then. As she turns back to me, her eyes begin to shine at the memory. "He filled the room. Right here. He didn't come through the door like you. He just materialised. A cloudy light. A strange feeling. And then there he was. I was really frightened—but he knew. The first thing he told me was not to be afraid."

"He gave me the same message," I say. "My angel, I mean. He said that I should not be afraid to take you as my wife because what was inside you was from the Holy Spirit."

Mary's hands go to the front of her slender body and rest there, her fingers extended.

Yes," she murmurs. "The angel told me that the child would be holy and would be called a Son of God."

"I take back every word of Reuben's message, Mary. Can you forgive my stupidity? You must have suffered so much. Will you let me make amends? I want so much to marry you, to love you, care for you, to make us a family. Will you still have me? Mary, will you marry me?"

Instead of answering, she simply gazes at me. But I can see a darkness clearing from her eyes. There is a tentative smile. I step closer to her, reaching out my hands towards her own.

"May I?" I ask her.

She nods, and I lay my hands over hers on her young body, where this child is beginning its life on earth. There is a strange little stifled laugh from her.

"There will be scandal," she murmurs. "Are you really sure you still want to marry me, Joseph?"

A scandal—yes, I think. There will be scandal. But I will not allow it to touch her. Her tender womb is rich with the Holy One to come. Awe overwhelms me, and I sink into a kneeling posture before her. She is a new tabernacle of the Lord.

"I'm absolutely sure," I say. "Will you have me for your husband, Mary?"

She begins to pull me to my feet and her lovely face gazes steadily into mine. "Yes," she speaks clearly. "I will, Joseph."

"Thank God," I breathe, and, rising from my knees, I take her in my arms and draw her close to me. I feel her body, warm, rich with the new and blessed life within her, held against mine. I mean this embrace as a promise to take care of her. From this day forward for ever and ever I will be her protector and cherish this mysterious unborn child within her. I feel her young tender body shake a little. She looks down. I have to tip her face up to mine to see into her eyes, lifting her chin with my fingers. She is struggling with pools of tears in her eyes, which, as I watch, tumble silently into rivulets down her flawless cheeks. I let her hide her face and dry her tears in the folds of my shirt.

Reflection

What a wondrous act of God this is, sending his Son to be born in flesh on our Earth through the womb of a young girl—a uniquely blessed young girl, perhaps, yet very ordinarily human too. What a revolution this divine act brings into Mary's and Joseph's lives! Mary hears the message once, and her assent changes everything from that moment. Joseph's journey is more tortuous in its beginning, leading him to the huge change of heart in this story. Initially, of course, he considered his decision in the light of the values and customs of his world, and with regard to his own feelings and his concern for Mary. Yet, once he has received the message from the angel, not for a moment doubting it to be from God, he is transformed.

He and Mary are alike in their unquestioning awe and obedience of God's angelic messengers. Both are united, not only in their love for one another, but in their total faith and trust in God. Despite all the worldly difficulties which lie in their path, they set out on their life's journey—a journey we shall follow with them through the Rosary.

Prayer

Lord, we praise and thank you for the gift of your Son to our earthly world. We thank you for the wonderful example of Mary and Joseph in their humble assent to your startling plan. May we always say yes, as they did, to your will for us. Let us pray that, like Joseph, we may not allow worldly values and considerations to dominate our decisions and our lives. Help us, Lord, to listen for your voice and to trust your prompting. Amen

2. The Visitation

There are lots of meetings in the Bible. Kings meet their advisors; prophets their people; Jesus meets the Pharisees; sinners seek him. But in this second Joyful Mystery, the meeting of Mary and Elizabeth, of two pregnant women, is unique.

One woman's husband has been left at home; the other's has been silenced by the Lord as a consequence of his doubts. These women meet alone, carrying their miraculous yet-to-be born children, fulfilling the will of God thereby, and poised on the very cusp of the most important change in human history. This story affirms the esteem, the huge value God places in women and the trust he has in them, in contrast to their contemporary culture, which held women in very low regard.

But this is our view of the story—looking back on the scene with the benefit of hindsight after seeing the wonderful outcome of these events. Perhaps to the young, inexperienced though faith-filled Mary, it all seemed rather different.

Hilltop Meeting

Mary allowed herself a rest near the well. She found a ledge of rock a convenient distance away, so she hindered no one's activities by sitting there. The well was roughly halfway up the hill from the village, so her travels were almost over. It was time to prepare herself to meet Elizabeth; but she craved a little time to herself before her journey ended. She had to dwell, just for a few last moments, on her own secret, on the promise made her by the Lord.

Yet, for a long time she was distracted by the people coming to the well for water. She watched them idly: women mostly, sometimes with children; two girls who came up the hill laughing together, perhaps sisters. It was approaching noon, and busy for such a quiet place; everyone trying to get this chore over before the hottest part of the day. She would come here every day from now on, she was thinking, to fetch water for her cousin Elizabeth. She resolved to come early in the morning when it was truly quiet. It might provide her with a time for prayer, which could be crowded out by all the caring and working activities of the rest of the day.

She turned and looked the other way into the trees. There were cooler shadows there, and some of the trees were hung with reddening pomegranates. The land rose from the valley at quite a steep gradient, rocky and untamed. It was good to be in hill country again. It had sometimes seemed an endless journey from the hills of Galilee. Step after step, mile after mile on long, level, hard-trodden roads across the desert lands.

"I'm surprised your husband sent you all this way on your own," some of her companions remarked on the road. Travellers joined together here, families, merchants going the same roads. Sometimes there would be quite a caravan for a few days together. It made the night camps safer, and often food was shared.

"I'm not alone," she wanted to say—but she held her tongue. She could not say that she had felt angels watching over her; it would have provoked too much curiosity. She should have told them—and she wasn't quite sure why she had not—that there had indeed been people accompanying her along parts of the way. Joseph himself at first, with the donkey, for as long as he could spare the time from work. And then he had arranged for two of his friends from further south to meet her later on—one of those lending her his mule for a while. Joseph, she knew, had really been anxious about her, but she had travelled before. She had climbed isolated mountain tracks, seeking the family's goats. She had assured him she was not afraid. And he himself had judged that she would be happier out of the public gaze of Nazareth for the coming months, and that she would be a blessing to her cousin, who might equally be a blessing for her.

Mary was not quite sure that she would prove the right company for her aged cousin, but she knew Elizabeth was now expecting her. She had been walking with a large family the last few days, and they had sent a boy on ahead to Ein-Kárem to set preparations in train for their accommodation. When they heard that Mary was related to Zechariah, who was quite famed in those parts, they volunteered the boy's services in alerting him to her imminent arrival. With some reluctance, she had agreed. When the boy returned, he told how Zechariah, unable to speak, had written on a tablet that his wife remained in their summer house at the top of the hillside, but would welcome her cousin Mary.

As she sat, gazing at last across the vast spaces between the hills and into the blue of the huge open sky, the glow of the mystery she held in her womb bloomed again within her. All through the troubles and the tedium of the journey, this one thing had outshone everything. It carried her, filled her. It was unlike anything she had ever known. She would not have believed it could have happened, but for the joy which filled every moment. Such joy! It somehow connected her in a new way with everything; as if she were part of the blue sky, and her blood ran in the sap of the trees, and her elation brushed everyone, like the breeze. She felt in love with everything. But especially with the coming child. She barely breathed the words, even silently inside her own head: that she was chosen to be the mother of the Son of God. She carried a new divine life within her own. She was to be the instrument that would bring about the fulfilment of her people's history. It was such a claim. She had told no one on the road. It would surely have been thought preposterous. Joseph had said it could be dangerous. Perhaps that was why she had not dared even to speak to them about Joseph. She had journeyed mostly in silence, wrapped in a powerful secret happiness of love. She hugged this treasure to herself now, a little sad that Joseph was not there to share in it and that it had to be kept so closely to herself, but filled far more strongly, overwhelmingly, with amazed thankfulness and awe. She gave silent thanks and praise to God.

At last, she upbraided herself. She must think of Elizabeth now. Her cousin's pregnancy was far more advanced than her own. And she was getting on in years; she must be in need of the help and energy of her younger cousin. Mary knew she must put her own concerns aside for a while and really be the greatest help she could to her cousin in the last weeks of what must surely be an ordeal. It was with determination to hold this resolution foremost in her mind that she rose at last to her feet and began the final section of the climb.

It was not long before she found Zechariah and Elizabeth's summer house. Doors in an archway in the wall stood wide open revealing an enclosed garden, and she could already see from the approaching track that Elizabeth was seated there awaiting her. As she drew nearer, she saw her older cousin begin to heave herself awkwardly to her feet. It was a timely reminder of her cousin's need, and she clutched at the sense of duty and family responsibility with which she had long been familiar.

As Elizabeth turned, still straightening from a stooped position, Mary stepped through the open doors onto the garden path.

"My dear cousin…" she began her greeting but fell abruptly silent as Elizabeth gave a sharp gasp, a cry, her hands moving to hold her swollen belly.

"Elizabeth?" Mary faltered, stopping in her tracks as well as in her planned little speech of greeting and offering of help. A spasm of alarm ran through her. Was Elizabeth in pain? But the older woman's initial gasp had given way to sighs and the sighs to something more musical: laughter, could it be? Mary held her breath, caught in uncertainty. When Elizabeth finally turned to her, rising to her full height and lifting her eyes to Mary's, her face was lit with such a smile—such wonder, such amusement—it astonished the younger woman.

"Such a leaping!" Elizabeth exclaimed. "What is this child to be?"

"My dear cousin," Mary said, moving closer, her relative's evident recovery not yet quite allaying her concern. "Shouldn't you sit down?" But Elizabeth reached out and took her hand, drew her nearer and laid the hand against her body where the child moved. There was a long pause held between them. Mary felt for herself the movement of her cousin's child. She lifted her eyes to Elizabeth's. There was warmth, excitement in them. Mary had not expected such a ready friendship, such sympathy. Something in her elderly cousin was so open and understanding.

"How blessed you are!" Elizabeth exclaimed, suddenly lifting her arms, palms upward. "Blessed above all other women. Blessed is the fruit of your womb!" Mary gazed at her in silence. She had not expected this.

"The fruit of my womb?" she echoed faintly, trying to remember what, if anything, Elizabeth might have heard.

"Why should I be honoured," her cousin continued, "with a visit from the mother of my Lord?" And taking both of Mary's hands in her own, she explained, "The moment your greeting reached my ears, the child in my womb leapt for joy. As if he knew. Yes, of course he knew—he knows, he knows the presence of the Lord. Yes, blessed is she who believed that the promise made her by the Lord would be fulfilled."

Mary's mind was adrift. She struggled to think clearly. She had been so conscientiously setting her mind on the duties of caring and the domestic tasks which awaited her, she had forgotten about the prophecies given concerning her cousin's child. The Lord had blessed Elizabeth too, of course. Elizabeth's child was an extraordinary gift of God, a promise made by the Lord, a miracle in her old age. A son. Could he already be gifted with awareness? Could he have recognised her own child as the Messiah to come? "You think he knew?" Mary murmured.

Elizabeth responded by embracing her slender cousin in her arms in a brief but forceful hug. "He's rejoicing!" she exclaimed, as she pulled away, but held Mary's shoulders at arms' length, the better to regard her. "Rejoicing at meeting his future cousin for whom he is to prepare the people's hearts. It was the angel's prophecy."

"I hadn't thought," said Mary, "so…"

"We were told he would be filled with the Holy Spirit."

"And the Holy Spirit knows everything!" gasped Mary. "Praise God!"

"Amen!"

"And you believe that I…"

"Are the most blessed of all women. The future mother of the Saviour."

Mary stared at her cousin. She took an enormous breath and breathed it out in laughter. "We two!" she gasped. "We are both blessed."

They were more than cousins, she was realising. They were sisters, or closer still. Two chosen by the Lord. It was like entering a different world. A huge relief, after all the secrecy she had imposed on herself. Floodgates opened within her. She could hold her joy within for not a moment longer; she must burst with the gift the Lord had granted her. She grasped her cousin's hands.

"My soul proclaims the greatness of the Lord!" she cried. "My spirit exults in God my Saviour. He has chosen me, his lowly handmaid, and done great things for me! All generations henceforth will call me blessed. Holy is his name!"

"Amen, amen," cried Elizabeth. "Holy is his name!"

"He has shown his mercy all down the ages to our people," Mary declared. "He has brought low the proud and blessed the lowly. He is keeping his promise to Israel—the promise made to Abraham and all generations. He is bringing their Saviour into the world."

"Thanks be to God," said Elizabeth, "for all he has done and all he will do in us."

"Thank you, my lovely cousin," Mary said. "It's so good to praise the Lord. I have had to keep quiet for so long."

"We can praise him every hour of every day," Elizabeth said. "While we nurture the gifts of the new lives he has granted us."

"We will," agreed Mary. "We will!"

"And we will dream and wonder at what the future holds for them and for all people."

Reflection

What a beautiful meeting this turns out to be! John the Baptist, still a growing child in his mother's womb, is stirred to such excitement by his closeness to the unborn Jesus Christ that he leaps in delight. In consequence, the meeting of these two women, graced by the Holy Spirit, likewise explodes into joy and thanksgiving to God. Separately, each had their own secret happiness, but when this comes to be shared, their joy and love of God knows no bounds. Mary breaks into her famous prayer of praise, the Magnificat.

These women are especially gifted, of course, with blessings from God of motherhood and children destined to be absolutely unique. But their joyful reaction to sharing these blessings with one another, and their union in praise and thanksgiving to God, can be an example and a beacon for us.

Prayer

Dear Lord, may we learn to imitate Mary and Elizabeth in sharing good news, and in praising and thanking you for all that you give us. They were graced by the presence and power of the Holy Spirit. May we too be open to the Holy Spirit in our lives. May he lead us, as he did John the Baptist while still unborn, into rejoicing in your presence amongst us. May he lead us into sharing all your gifts with others, so that more and more will join together in praise of your wisdom and love. Amen

3. The Nativity of Jesus

This, the third Joyful Mystery, encompasses so much. It holds the entire Christmas story, the coming, the arrival of the Messiah as a vulnerable human child. The King of all space and time born in flesh in the humble poverty of an outhouse, or perhaps a cave, sharing the straw bedding of animals. God coming to walk on our Earth, stepping down from his eternal Glory into the narrow confines of a human life as man and God, united and inseparable.

Perhaps our minds are incapable of ever really comprehending the immensity of this event. Certainly, no simple storytelling could embrace its fullness. But it changed lives. From the very beginning it transformed lives. So perhaps if we think about just one life...

In the stable

My sister Lydia was never strong. They tell me she was sickly as a baby. The midwife warned that she would not live long. I was too young then, of course, to understand. She survived into childhood, though, despite the sad predictions. But she was always pale and spindly, like a plant deprived of sunlight. I, her older brother by three years, must have seemed all the more beefy by comparison.

When we grew beyond early childhood, and I was about twelve, it was always expected that I would help with any hard physical labour, unloading carts, shifting casks, stacking furniture. I didn't usually mind. Lydia was so patently a weakling. Her eyes seemed dark and huge in her tiny heart-shaped face. Her complexion was like milk. But she had this amazing copper-coloured hair. Mine was dark like mother's. Father's was light brown. There were uncles in our family with reddish hair, apparently, but they had died. Lydia was not like anyone else.

She wasn't lazy. She tried to carry the pails out and to feed the hens. But sometimes even that was beyond her strength. She helped mostly with the sewing. She turned sheets so they lasted longer or mended our clothes. And she had a vast imagination. She could gaze at night skies, or daydream in the synagogue with her eyes closed for hours. She had an eye for beautiful things.

Sometimes it was thanks to her that I noticed them at all. The colours in the clouds, the dappling of water, the patterns in the wood grain of our stools and tables.

Lydia was always telling us her dreams. They were rambling fantasies that we listened to mainly just to humour her. So, we never took much notice when she told us she'd had this dream about a baby. We got on with the daily business of running the inn. It was mother who noticed that she was slowly creating a small patchwork quilt out of scraps of fabric saved from here and there. She had been meticulously gathering feathers from the henhouse too, sometimes washing them in the trough in an old muslin bag.

"What's that you're making?" our mother asked.
"A special blanket," my sister answered, "for the baby that's coming."
"What baby?"
Lydia sighed. "The baby that's coming. I don't know exactly. I just know he's very special and he's coming here."
"And how do you know that?" my father enquired. Lydia simply raised her hands in a gesture of mysterious unknowing.

We had all seen this kind of strange behaviour before. Had she been stronger, my parents would probably have knocked it out of her, setting her to daily chores in the yard or over the washtub. But her frailty gave her a way out of all that. Father shook his head and let her alone. Mother said it was very pretty, but perhaps she would not forget the towels that needed hemming. And to do my sister justice, she did set the patchwork aside, and take up the towels instead.

Passover was usually our busiest time. But when the census was called, and all those of the house of David had to be registered here in Bethlehem, we had the busiest time of all. The rooms were all taken early. Even the alcoves and corridors filled up with those prepared to sleep on just a patch of floor for a lesser price. I was despatched to the market umpteen times for extra supplies. The kitchen filled with steam and cooking smells and dirty platters, and even with all our extra workers in, people got impatient at the tables.

It was very late in the evening. Most of the extra help had left and mother was exhausted. While father was still busy fetching up new barrels, there was knocking at the yard door. I left the jugs and tables to go and answer it. I heard mother shout that I should send them away.

"We're full, I'm afraid," I said to the couple of travellers who stood in the darkness, their features hardly lighted by the lamplight from the doorway. He was tall, cloaked, angular. His hand held the bridle of a donkey, which still bore on its back the figure of a woman. From the turn of her head, she seemed young, yet her shoulders were stooped.

"Is there nowhere?" the man asked. He gestured to his wife. "She's with child. She needs rest. Perhaps in the stable with the donkey? We've asked everywhere."

"Wait there," I said, astonished at the request, but convinced of their desperation. "I'll ask."

When I reported this to father, he asked me to take over, while he went to the door. He was away for quite a while. "Did you put them in the stable?" I asked when he returned.

He nodded. "Had to. Not a spare inch inside. That girl looks near her time. Take them bread and water, Simon, would you, when you get the chance?"

I went down the yard some time later with a lantern. It made shadows move among the cobblestones, as if they were alive. I could hear a low moaning as I drew close. The man came out to meet me, looking anxious at first, and then pleased at the sight of the loaf of bread and the pitcher I was bringing.

"Are you all right in there?" I asked.

"We'll be fine. Someone's fetching a midwife. It's good of you to bring this out to us at this hour."

"I wish we could have fitted you inside," I said, "but they're packed in everywhere."

He shook his head as he took the pitcher from me and turned back to his wife. "Thanks for this," he called, holding the bread aloft, as I stepped back with the lantern.

Then I had second thoughts. I went after him into the stable doorway and set the lantern down on the stone floor. I could sense the woman's presence, rather than see her. I didn't like to look at her directly. "Keep this," I said, and turned to make my way back up the familiar yard again in total darkness.

Later that night, I tossed and turned on my mattress, trying to sleep, but thinking of the couple who were lying in the straw of the stable. Was their baby really being born this night, out in the stable, among the animals? Then I remembered what Lydia had said about a baby. Perhaps this was what she'd dreamt. Could she really have dreams that came true?

We were up betimes, to get the ovens heated and bread baked for another busy day. With all the clearing left from late the night before and all the chaos of departing guests with bills to settle, it was broad daylight before I had a chance to explain to my sister what had happened. Mother had put some leftovers in a pot for me to take to her unexpected stable guests.

"Wait," shrieked Lydia. "Wait for me. I'm coming with you." But she turned into the house. I guessed it was the patchwork creation she was fetching for the baby. I stood in the doorway, waiting for her, rather dreading the embarrassment of seeing Lydia boldly entering the stable to present them with her gift. Maybe the baby wasn't even born yet, or maybe something had gone wrong. These things happened. I was old enough at least to know that.
"Is it all right?" I asked mother, as Lydia returned, clutching her little quilt in both hands. Mother only shrugged.

So, we went down the yard together. Halfway there, both of us hesitated. We could hear the sound of voices. Men's voices, from the stable, full of laughter. Lydia and I looked at one another, and then pushed on to the stables, united and impelled by curiosity. The stable doors were open wide. Lydia rushed ahead, but we both stopped in the entrance. I stood behind her, staring at them, as they looked up, startled, and stared at us.

In the stable's wooden manger, in the middle of the floor, was a tiny, swaddled baby on a bed of straw. The new mother, with a peaceful smile, was seated close to one side, resting on a bale of hay, while the father stood beside her. I could see their faces properly now by daylight. Both of them seemed lit with joy. On the other side of this improvised cot were three men, shepherds, by the look of them, in rough tunics and cloaks. One was old, white-haired and held a shepherd's crook; one was plump with a dark beard; the third was not much older than me. All of them shared the same look of incredible joy. I couldn't think what to say.

But Lydia hardly hesitated. She went forward, holding out the little coloured quilt she had made. "It's for the baby," she explained. "I knew you'd come."

"Did you see the angels, too?" asked the young shepherd boy.

"Angels?" said my sister, stopped in her tracks, turning to him.

"They came to us in the fields," said the boy. "To tell us the great news."

"News?" I questioned.

The bearded shepherd smiled. "That a saviour had been born in the city of David," he said. "They told us we'd find him wrapped in swaddling clothes and lying in a manger."

"And that's just how we found him," declared the boy.

"A saviour?" I repeated.

"We heard the choirs of angels singing," said the old one, raising his bony face as if to heaven. "And a great light shone from the sky."

"It was terrifying, but they told us not to be afraid," said the boy. "They said it was news of great joy for all the world. That this newborn is our Messiah and Lord."

I knew they were telling the truth. There was something about them. I looked from them to the tiny new child. A Saviour? Could it be? But who was I to doubt?

I looked at the parents. There was such peace in their smiles. The mother reached out her hand to the manger. "I saw an angel too," she said, gently. "I was told this child would be holy. We are to call him Jesus."

"Praise God," said the plump shepherd, his eyes shining.

"Praise God," echoed the others. "Glory to Him, for ever and ever."

Lydia took a step towards the baby. "May I?" she asked.

"Please," said the mother of the newborn Lord.

So, Lydia went right up to the manger, and gently placed her quilt onto the child. She tucked in the edges. Then she knelt down and bent her head.

I suddenly felt the hot pricking of tears in my eyes, and the scene went misty. My sister—the sickly child, the one we thought we had to humour and support—she was so much wiser than I. She knew, not only that this special child would come here but how to behave. There was I standing like an oaf, while she knelt humbly, gracefully, in prayer. Her hair shone like gold.

"Praise God," I stammered and sank awkwardly down onto my knees, the cooking pot bumping onto the ground before me. I had forgotten all about it. "Oh… my mother sent you this," I explained, lifting it clumsily towards them.

The father took it from me. "Thank you," he said, in a deep and beautiful voice. "And thank you for not closing the door last night. Your kindness won't be forgotten."

His words seemed to blow away my awkward self-consciousness, like chaff in the wind. I did belong here, after all. Lydia twisted round to give me a smile. I realised that all the shepherds were following her example too. They got down on their knees before the crib.

Something held us there in silence for long moments. Something that filled our hearts and made tears swim in my eyes. Strange tears of happiness. Everything seemed right. We were sharing something together. Sharing in a secret that was going to spread throughout the world. Sharing a secret which would change the world, as it had already changed me.

I would never see my little sister as a weakling again. She had a different kind of strength. Something which came up from a deeper place than the strength of muscle and bone.

Reflection

Simon, son of the innkeeper, a young working lad, here finds his mind and heart opened in a new way. His sister, previously considered a weakling, proves the catalyst in bringing him into a new revelation of wonder. His view of his sister is turned upside down. Yet the greatest change is in the nature of his faith.

Perhaps he went regularly and reverently with his family to the synagogue and considered himself a believer in God. Yet this is clearly something new. For the first time perhaps, he comes to know the reality of the presence of God right here on Earth. He kneels in worship and in tears at this new sense of life. The presence of the Holy Family and the Christ-child transforms him.

In this Mystery, we begin to see the impact of God's coming to Earth as fully man and fully divine. Christ humbled himself, as the liturgy tells us, to take on our humanity, so that we might share in his divinity. We should be awed, like Simon, at this extraordinary blessing.

Prayer

Father in heaven, we pray that we, like Simon, may come to know you as a very real presence in our lives. We thank you for sending us the precious gift of your only Son, Jesus, not as a mighty and powerful God-figure, but incarnate, as one of us—as a helpless child born in a stable. May we be awoken from our token or shallow faith into profound wonder and reverence at your presence here on Earth—indeed in our very lives. Through this Mystery of the Rosary, may we imitate Mary in bringing Christ to birth in our own hearts. May a deepening faith help us to touch others, as Lydia did, and thus spread an awareness of how real you are. Amen

4. The Presentation of Jesus in The Temple

What contrasts there are in this story! Between the youthfulness of Mary with her very new baby, and the great age of Anna and Simeon. Between the breathless pace of change in the lives of Mary and Joseph, and the steady, patient endurance of these elders of the Temple. Between the fresh, new complexion of the child, Jesus, and the aged hands and grizzled beard of Simeon.

It is like a meeting of two worlds. Yet it is not a scene of conflict. It is a scene of amazing understanding and harmony. It forms a bridge between the times of the Old and the New Testaments. And this time, as we look back on these events, the view from the perspective of our times is not entirely different from the view of the participants at the time. At different levels, perhaps, all of them had an awareness of the significance of what was happening. But maybe it came a little more slowly to some than others.

Simeon's Voice

He was an old friend, of course, a dear friend, and I shouldn't really have minded his raised voice disturbing my devotions. But I am old and set in my ways, and I'm sorry to say that a definite spasm of annoyance went through me at the invasion of my prayers by the distinctive tones of Simeon coming from within the temple. For a while I persisted, going back to the words of the psalm, and beseeching the Lord to have mercy on his people Israel. Truly I yearned for the restoration of the rule of the Almighty in our land; I had dedicated my life to prayer in this cause. I tried to concentrate, to keep myself within the flame the Lord had lighted in my heart, and to listen for his words.

Alas! The words that reached me were those of Simeon. Not the words exactly—they echoed through the temple archways, and I could not make them out clearly—but the tone of his voice struck me forcibly. Not only was it loud, there was some unusual excitement in it. With a sudden flash, the thought came. Perhaps this was what the Lord wanted me to hear. I was getting too old for surprises, but this one suddenly gained a new importance. I made an apology to the Lord for breaking off, rose from my knees, gathered my draped shawl in one hand, held my long skirt before me with the other to avoid tripping over its hems, and began to make my way towards the noise.

Simeon was a good man. He could not match me in age, but he was pretty well on in years and lived a devout life here in Jerusalem, longing as I did for an end to foreign occupation and for the dawn of a new age. He came by the temple quite frequently and we often talked together, even prayed together. Like me, he felt he received guidance from the Holy Spirit.

Sometimes we shared our experiences. He had once told me of a wonderful and remarkable prophecy made to him one night when he had not been able to sleep and had risen from his bed. He was on his knees, near the window of his house, gazing at a wealth of stars in the black sky above Jerusalem's housetops. A voice sounded in his ears. He knew there was no person nearby. The voice was almost inside him. "You will not see death," the voice declared, "until you have set eyes on the Messiah of the Lord."

How we celebrated those words! The Messiah—in our lifetime! Or at least in Simeon's lifetime, which surely could not extend too many years beyond mine. So, it was close; it would be within this generation! The arrival of a new Messiah! Maybe we would both live to see the establishment of a new kingdom. The restoration of the true kingdom of Israel. We were breathless with excitement.

Some years had passed now, of course, since those days of heady anticipation. The excitement had waned a little. But we were wise enough to know that times of waiting were significant. We rededicated ourselves to our devotions and let the days pass slowly, praising the Lord for all his great gifts, thanking him for the promise made to Simeon, and praying for the future of our people and our land.

I could make out the broad figure of Simeon now, but he was with others, and they stood against the light, so the group was one of dark silhouettes. The others in the group were slighter in build than Simeon, but impossible to recognise at this distance.

The thought of Simeon's prophecy had come to the surface of my mind, naturally, and briefly I had allowed myself to wonder if there could be some news of its fulfilment, some message perhaps. But rapidly I had repressed the thoughts. It was hardly likely to come on a quiet, ordinary kind of day like this one, after all. There would be signs, miracles, announcements of some kind.

It would be known everywhere, surely. And I reminded myself of Simeon's growing deafness. It made his speech more emphatic than was necessary. Probably a couple of strangers had wandered into the temple precincts and were asking his advice, which Simeon could enthusiastically and amply provide. No doubt that was what he was doing.

As I drew closer, something in the expression of the strangers must have alerted Simeon to my approach, because my steps were silent. I loved to live in silence. But Simeon turned and saw me. "Anna," he greeted me. "Anna, this is a great day."

"Indeed," I said, coming up close to the little group, and discerning a man and a young woman with a very small child bundled in her arms. Two of the temple virgins were just turning away with two turtledoves in a small cage, which the couple had evidently brought as their gift. I knew at once that they had come to bring their firstborn to be consecrated to the Lord. "A great day indeed," I repeated, smiling at the couple who had this wonderful gift of a child from the Lord.

"No, Anna, you don't understand," Simeon spoke with huge emphasis. For a moment, I glanced anxiously at the couple, not wanting their day to be spoilt by any strange behaviour from Simeon. He must have seemed a little unworldly by their standards. But they surprised me; their faces looked strangely rapt. I glanced back at Simeon.

"I had no intention of visiting the temple today, you see," Simeon explained to me. "But something in my heart made me change my mind. There was an urge, a driving compulsion within me, which I could not disobey. I had to come here. And when I did, I met these good people. Joseph and Mary." He indicated each in turn with his hand, and I made a little bow to each in greeting.

"And this is their boy-child, whom they wish to call Jesus."

The name startled me. "Jesus?" I questioned.

"It is what the angel told us," Mary spoke quietly. "He said that we must name him Jesus and that he would be called the Son of the Most High."

Simeon took a huge breath and beamed at me. He was aglow. I was still trying to grasp what had been said. An angel had told them to call this child 'one who saves'? He was to be 'the Son of the Most High'? I couldn't quite take that step into belief that Simeon had so obviously taken. A part of my mind was thinking there must be more of a fanfare, surely, more people…

"He is the one we have waited for," Simeon declared. "May I?" He held out his arms towards the child. The young mother lifted her baby into the old man's arms. Simeon took him gratefully, gently, and turned him a little to enable me to see. With his strong fingers he delicately shifted the clothing from near the child's face, and suddenly we could both see the face of a tiny baby. He gazed back at us. A steady regard from bright eyes, set in a complexion so fine and soft it touched my heart with a sudden instinctive love for one so beautiful. I drew an astonished breath. "Praise you, Lord for the gift of this child," Simeon intoned, in his huge voice. "Praise you for this glorious day." Then he raised the baby a little and held him out in front of us between his gnarled hands.

We gazed in silence. Excitement prickled within me. As if sparks were lighting something new in my heart. The face of this child seemed so bright and clear. I saw nothing else. Simeon, the parents, the building, all had suddenly been submerged into fog. And there was such peace in his face. And something more. There was a sort of gentle depth in the darkness of those eyes; as if the child not only looked out at us but welcomed us to enter into his world. He was such a tiny, helpless, newborn child, yet a torch flared in my heart, and I trembled before him.

"Praise to you, Lord, and glory," I stammered, unsteady on my feet now, with the shock of realising my own doubting arrogance. I sank awkwardly onto my knees, both humbled and awed by a huge certainty that this child was divine. My body trembled.

"Now, Master," said Simeon, lowering his arms and holding the holy child closer to himself, almost against his full, grey beard. "You can let your servant go in peace, just as you promised; because my eyes have seen the salvation which you have prepared. Salvation for all the nations to see, a light to enlighten the pagans and the glory of your people Israel."

Simeon's words caught in my mind: 'for all the nations'. They were the words given to Isaiah. So not just for Israel? A Saviour for the whole world? Of course. My mind whirled. How God never ceases to surprise us! His plans are more immense than we can conceive, and his means so much smaller than we can imagine. I felt humbled before God.

Simeon was handing back the child, and the young woman had stepped closer to take her son from the big, aged hands of Simeon into her own slender arms. It was then, when she came closer to me, and I looked up from my kneeling posture into her face, that a flash of recognition struck me. Mary. Of course. I had known her as a child. She was only a little changed, taller, the jawline more defined. She had spent time in her childhood as one of the temple virgins, and I was among those who had taught her and cared for her in those days. "Mary!" I exclaimed softly, still on my knees.

She glanced at me and gave a smile. "You remember me?" she asked.

"Of course," I replied, remembering everything. She had always struck me as a remarkable child. One with a strangely natural holiness. She had a simplicity of manner, and a strength of faith which were unusual. And God had chosen her to mother his own Son!

"What an honour the Lord has conferred on you!" I exclaimed. "And what an honour that he has brought you here to us, that we should be gifted with the sight of this…" but words failed me. There were no words I could find to express my amazement, that God should bring his great Messiah to Earth in this quiet and unpretentious way, and that we should be the earliest witnesses.

Mary was silent a moment, and then she raised an arm towards me. "Oh, please," she said, with a gestured sign that I should rise from my knees. But I stayed as I was. My frame was weak, and my limbs trembled. I knew I could not stand. And in penance for my doubts and in worship of this miraculous Son of God, it seemed the only appropriate way to be.

"Then I shall kneel too," she said, coming closer, kneeling at my side, holding her baby in one arm, and lifting the other to me, to place a hand lovingly on my shoulder.

Simeon raised his hand in blessing, and Joseph joined us too, kneeling before him. "May God bless you both and keep you," Simeon pronounced. "May he grant you all the gifts and graces you will need as mother and father to this blessed infant."

Then he bent his head to Mary. "You see this child," he spoke in lowered tones, more confidential, but still extremely audible. "He is destined for the fall and for the rising of many in Israel, destined to be a sign that is rejected, and a sword will pierce your own soul too so the secret thoughts of many will be laid bare."

I saw a cast of alarm cross Mary's face at these words. Cradling the child with both arms now, she looked round at Joseph, her husband. He put his arm around her, and the anxious look faded, though her eyes remained wide. She stared questioningly at Simeon. But he had his eyes almost closed as if in prayer. I knew he was asking for a further explanation of this pronouncement, which I did not doubt Simeon had uttered in all sincerity, and in obedience to the prompting of the Spirit.

Mary turned to look at me, but a chill had crossed my heart as well, and I knew no more than she of the purport of these words. I kept silence. I would pray for her. Daily, I resolved, I would pray for her.

As I made an effort to give a comforting smile, there came a sudden cry from the baby. He stirred, wriggled within his mother's embrace, his hands waving in the air. Mary resettled him, looking down into his face. Then she lowered her head so that her cheek touched his. The cry softened into murmuring. When Mary looked up again, her face had relaxed into the gaze of maternal love. It took away the cold shadow of Simeon's prophecy. I saw that she would be the best of all mothers.

"We should go in," Simeon said, "to complete the ceremony and the law's fulfilment."
"Yes," said Joseph. "We will follow you."

So Simeon, with no more words, led the way further into the temple, and Mary and Joseph with this tiny child who bore the weight of so much prophecy and expectation, obediently followed. I had risen slowly, with the help of Joseph's proffered hand, and now, rather unsteadily, I brought up the rear of our little procession, my heart full and my mind tumbling with all these events. I could barely put it into words: Mary was the chosen instrument of God to bring his own Son into this world. How blessed she was! And I had lived to see this day!

It would take a long time before I could reflect quietly on all the meaning and on the consequences of this day. But I knew it would change us all for ever. And despite the chilling effect of Simeon's prophecy, my heart in its depth was rejoicing. Our Messiah had come. Not, perhaps, as we had expected.

God's ways are not our ways. There had been no grand announcements, no preparations, no ceremony. But salvation was at hand all the same. God would fulfil his promise to our people. And it was up to us to tell everyone the news. We were honoured and blessed too. I gave thanks and glory to the Lord and followed them in silence.

Reflection

Anna's life moves at a slow pace, in silence. Perhaps it is because of this, as well as her conventional expectations of a triumphal entry of the Messiah into the world, that, in this story at least, she is a little slow to recognise the presence of the Son of God. Compared with the length of Anna's life, however, this is but a momentary delay before the full significance of what is happening fully dawns upon her. She realises that this is indeed, as Simeon already knows, the fulfilment of the prophecy made to him. She is overwhelmed by the presence, although in unexpected form, of the awaited Saviour. Even so, she recognises Mary. She remembers being aware of an extraordinary faith in Mary when she knew her as a child. She notices her gifts: her sensitive maternal love and her obedience to God and the Temple ways as she consecrates her child to God. Anna provides us with a revealing window onto the events of this Mystery: the new motherhood and dedication of Mary and the first public recognition of the birth of God's long-prophesied Messiah.

Prayer

Eternal Father, Mary, our Blessed Lady, gives us a powerful example of faithful surrender in the way she brings her most precious child to consecrate him to you. She gives him to you for your blessing and for you to guide according to your purpose. Help us, too, Father, to offer all we have to you. Help us to surrender our hopes, plans and dreams into your care. May we also, like Anna, live lives of faith and allow the miracle of your incarnation to fill us with the light of wonder and transform our minds and hearts. Amen

5. The Finding of Jesus in The Temple

The part of this story which strikes home with most of us is not so much the "finding" but the terror of losing the child, Jesus—or indeed any child. Most parents will, to a greater or lesser extent, have experienced the moments, or sometimes hours, of panic at the sudden unexplained loss of the presence of their child. All of us surely can empathise with Mary. Do we have the same sympathy for Joseph? Do we think about how it must have seemed to him? Jesus was not his own natural son, after all. Did it make a difference?

Journey in Fatherhood

You know everything, Lord. I kneel here before you. You know my failings, but I desire to bring them to you all the same. You placed such trust in me, and I so deeply repent, Lord, of the complacent thoughtlessness which brought us to the very brink of disaster.

I should have been more vigilant, dear Lord, of the child and of the mother you placed in my care. You know how weak I am. That day I wasn't even thinking.

When Jesus was born, there was so much upheaval and change. So many dramatic revelations, so many ways in which our lives were turned upside down—or perhaps turned the right way up, in truth. Even after all the amazement of his conception and birth, there was the terrible edict from Herod and the necessity for us to flee into Egypt and live there in exile, waiting on news of the king's death. We were vigilant then. But once we had returned and settled in our home in Nazareth, life took on a more regular and gentle character. We had our own place in the world, and our son grew up alongside his peers, among our relatives and friends, like any other child. We did not speak about his origins, not wanting people to talk or draw attention to him. It seemed best to bring him up like all the other boys and teach him my trade of carpentry. Whatever his future held, he would be able to support himself and be independent, should anything happen to us.

We had a long, settled and wonderful period during his childhood. After the early traumas, we loved its calm and quietness. We watched our child's every development with doting affection. We treasured his first steps, his first words, the lengthening limbs, the darkening hair—even the first bruises!

He made (with much help) a little stool in my workshop, with only one bruise, when he dropped a hammer on his foot! There was no lasting damage, and the pain that made him howl at least taught him to keep the tools well away from the edges of tables. As the years passed, he grew taller, of course, and became a small person instead of a baby. He was good-natured. He liked to help me in my work if he could, and eventually he grew old enough to run errands and make himself useful to neighbours and friends.

We were proud of him. I was a very proud father, as if he were my own. I thought of him as my son. Truly, I think sometimes we almost forgot the prophecies that had been made about him, forgot that he was not of my begetting. Yes, we drifted into a state of forgetful and tranquil security. (Forgive us, dear Lord in heaven.)

So, when we were returning home after the Feast of the Passover in Jerusalem and Jesus was not with us, danger was the last thing on our minds. We were in a large caravan of returning people and families stretched along the road, and some mixing of groups was perfectly normal. We presumed our boy was with his own friends or with relatives. Mary and I walked side by side, carefree, sometimes silent, thinking our own thoughts, and sometimes enjoying sporadic chatter with other folk. It was only as the darkness began to fall towards the end of the first day's journey that Mary remarked on Jesus' absence.

"Well, he's older now, don't forget," I said, without a qualm. "He probably prefers the company of his own friends."

Mary accepted this in silence. The evening wore on, still without an appearance from our son, and we began to settle, like a good many others, beneath a copse of trees to camp for the night. We thought he would appear at this point, but we were still on our own when we lay down to sleep.

We found we were still on our own the following morning.

"It's not like him, Joseph," Mary said.

"No," I agreed, feeling a faint prickling of alarm myself. But I told myself to be sensible—not to be so easily panicked. "I expect he was with friends all day yesterday," I said. "Probably with Shem and Matthew, Malachi's boys. Maybe they couldn't locate us in the dark, so Malachi thought it best for him to spend the night with them."

Mary considered this but shook her head. "It's just not like him."

"He'll be all right," I insisted, despite my own feelings. "He is twelve years old, after all."

When the morning was fully light, and our few possessions had been repacked and we started again on the road, I noticed that Mary was constantly looking round, trying to spot our boy among the crowd. I looked too, but more surreptitiously, to avoid alarming her. The effort proved vain.

After an hour or so, Mary took hold of my arm, and looked up at me with anxious eyes. "Go and see, would you, Joseph? Find Malachi and ask him. Search, please, would you? Find our boy?"

It was what I wanted to do anyway. "Of course I will, if you're so worried," I agreed. "But I'm sure he's fine."

So, I spent that morning, sometimes striding to get ahead of the crowd, sometimes standing watching as the straggling, lengthy caravan of people returning from Jerusalem went by, and I looked everywhere among the family groups, the animals, the carts, the young, the old, for Jesus. And sometimes, seeing someone I knew, I joined their group and questioned them—had they seen our boy? Had they seen Jesus anywhere?

When I found Mary again, without bringing home our son, she was distraught. Tears welled in her eyes. "Where could he be? Oh Joseph! What could have happened?"

"We'll find him," I said. "Of course we'll find him."

"You're worried too," Mary said. I nodded. There must have been a shake in my voice which gave me away. "I'll come with you," said Mary. "We'll search together. We have to find him."

So together, and with mounting anxiety, we searched all afternoon. We found Malachi's family at last, ahead of the caravan, but they gazed at us in surprise. Jesus was not with them.

"Have you seen him on the journey at all?" Mary questioned, out of breath. "Have you seen him since we set out?"

The two young boys shook their heads. The parents looked concerned, but their sympathy only helped to intensify our fears.

There was a twist of dread now in the pit of my stomach. My mind, despite my efforts, was thinking of all the fearful things that might have happened. I was as desperate as Mary to know where he was; perhaps more desperate, because I should have been a responsible father. Fine father I made! I couldn't help remembering the days when I had thought, with the help of your grace, Lord, I could be a good father to the child. How foolish that looked now. Had we lost him? Had some accident befallen him? Had someone evil, knowing his true nature, somehow stolen him away—or worse? In our selfish enjoyment of his childhood, my responsibility to look after him had been forgotten! Why had we not thought to check on the boy's whereabouts earlier? Why had I been so thoughtless?

When we were alone again, Mary held my arm and drew me to a stop. "We have to go back," she cried. "He isn't in the caravan, is he?"

"All right," I agreed. I didn't need much persuading. The consequences of not finding Jesus were too huge even to contemplate. I simply could not bear to think of it. "We'll turn back. We'll retrace our steps to Jerusalem."

Mary gave a great sigh. She had expected me to resist. I had been too slow to sympathise. All my mistakes were overwhelming me. Had we lost everything? I knew we needed your divine help. How quick we are to turn to you when things go wrong, Lord. I should have prayed to you long before. I should be constantly seeking your guidance.

"Let's kneel and pray, first," I said.
"Yes," she agreed.

So that is what we did. Within the shelter of a little dip at the side of the road, we knelt together before you, our almighty God. We prayed that we might somehow and somewhere find this precious son—your Son, who had been entrusted into our care. We prayed for your forgiveness for our foolish carelessness. We implored you to guide us to wherever Jesus was. We begged you to speed our steps. We prayed for our son's safety, for people to be near him who could help him. We prayed the most earnest prayers of our life. And then we ate and drank before the journey and set out to walk in the opposite direction to everyone else.

It took us the rest of that day and the next to cover the distance back to Jerusalem. People in the long procession of travellers held us up at first, asking why we were going the wrong way. It hampered our progress, but we did not dare to ignore their interest. Who knew if they might not have seen something which would give us an idea of what had become of our child?

Poor Mary was exhausted by the fast pace we felt compelled to keep up, but refused to stop and rest, except for the few hours we slept under a grove of trees during the night.

"It doesn't matter if I'm tired, Joseph," she replied, packing up our night things, when I protested that she should rest for longer. "Nothing matters except that we must find Jesus."

In Jerusalem it was hard to know where to begin. We searched the streets we had travelled down as we left the city, calling at inns or houses on the way, questioning passers-by. We went to the house where we had stayed during the festival with a relative, and then to other friends' houses. Jesus was nowhere to be found.

"We need to pray," I said, too weary myself now to walk much further, and thinking, in my concern for Mary, that this might be one way to make her rest. "We'll go to the Temple," Mary said.

So it was that we passed wearily through the Temple gates and made our way across its open square, its light stone blazing in the late afternoon sun, eventually entering the shady, cool and quiet interior. Slowly now, and with quiet steps, we walked along the wide, arched passageway deeper into the Temple, as we had done so many years ago, following Simeon.

Suddenly, Mary clutched my arm. I stopped and turned to her. But I had already guessed what had returned to her mind. "The words of Simeon," she whispered. "Do you remember?"

I was about to make a reply about our minds following the same course, but just then I heard a sound of distant voices. So, I nodded instead, and laid a finger on her lips, to quiet her. "Listen," I whispered.

From a distance, we heard a deep, steady voice, speaking for some time, and then a second, and a third, breaking in as if they were making objections or arguments in a serious discussion. And then there was a lighter voice. A child's voice.

Mary took to her heels, running with a sudden new energy along the stone floors, around corners, seeking out the sound. I followed close behind. After a few moments, an archway on the right opened to reveal a lighted chamber within. A group of men were seated round on benches in the lamplight, their faces toward us. Young but serious, thoughtful faces suggested they were learned scholars, doctors perhaps. Facing them, on a stool, his back turned to us, sat our long-lost son. The small figure was unmistakeable.

A strange cry broke from Mary's throat, and I saw all the men's heads lift in alarm, as she flew across the chamber and almost fell at her son's feet, her arms clutching him in an embrace. Jesus looked round and saw me. His face was one of astonishment. "My child," Mary cried, "why have you done this to us? Your father and I have been so worried looking for you."

As the doctors rose to their feet in consternation, I drew closer and placed a hand on each of them, my dear wife and my dear son, overwhelmed with thankfulness at this reunion.

"You have no idea, my son," I gasped, somewhat breathless still, "how relieved we are to find you! Your mother is exhausted. We were alarmed at the thoughts of what might have happened to you."

Jesus still looked uncomprehending. "Why were you looking for me?" he asked. "Did you not know that I must be busy with my Father's affairs?"

The shock in our faces must have shocked him. He looked suddenly daunted and a little pale. My mind was stunned. And then thoughts swirled around— amazing thoughts. They left me speechless.

I had lost this child you put into my care, Lord, but you—you had found him, called him to this place and kept him safe from harm. Not only was this a heartbreaking reminder of my own shortcomings, and of your—his true Father's—deep and ceaseless love. But he knew! Jesus knew he was the Son of God! How often had Mary and I earnestly discussed the problem of when we should explain to him exactly who he was? How often had we asked ourselves when he would be old enough to understand? How often had we talked about the best way we could help our boy through the process of coming to grasp the role that you had planned for him? And now… I stared at Jesus. Everything was changed.

"Your Father's affairs?" Mary's faint voice echoed her son's words, her tone one of wonderment. I knew she had the same stumbling thoughts as mine. Jesus coloured a little and turned his face away.

"My son," I pronounced at last, abandoning the maelstrom of realisations, and regathering my strength. "Your mother and I have been desperately searching for you for days. You should not leave us for so long without letting us know where you will be."

"He has been safe here." One of the scholars came across to offer reassurance. "So, he's your boy? And you didn't realise he was here?"

I nodded in assent.

"He has a remarkable mind in one so young. He has talked with us here with more insight than many grown men. You should be proud."

I made a little bow to him in acknowledgment, too shocked to reply. But Mary was recovering herself more quickly.

"Thank you, sir," she answered him. "We are certainly proud of him, but he is still a child."

"Indeed. A gifted child, I think. It is good you care so much for him. Well, Jesus," he went on, turning to our son. "You must go with your mother and father now. You must let them take you home." He turned to me once more.

"He would be welcome here, however, when you are visiting the city again. He can teach us things, I think."

"Really?" Mary responded; her eyes wide with new perceptions.

"A part of me belongs here, that's all," Jesus spoke up. "I'm sorry if it worried you."

His mother and I exchanged glances. Behind the shock there was the beginning of a smile in Mary's expression. I knew my face was the same. We had found our son! There was much to learn about him, but our fears were ended.

"Praise and thank you, Lord," Mary said as we walked out of the Temple, with Jesus between us.

"Amen," I agreed. "We will never stop praising and thanking you!"

It was a new and different journey then. We walked, the three of us, with new energy and with new joy. We praised and rejoiced. There were no questions. No recriminations. It was a blessed, special time of relief, peace and happiness. Jesus was safe again and skipped between us from time to time. We were on our way home.

It is now, my God, that I come before you to face up to things. We have been home a few days: days filled, for me, like restless seas, with the powerful currents of shifting assessments and thoughts about what happened. Days filled with a deepening knowledge of my own unworthiness. But also, with a deeper and more awesome sense of your power, your love, your mysterious plan.

I am nothing, Lord God, but you are with me. You have given me my blessed wife, my beloved Mary, and given to both of us the wondrous task of bringing up your Son. I bless you Lord, for the trust you have placed in us. I bless you, Lord, for the rescue you brought about, when we let you down. And I crave your mercy, dear God, for all my faults and failings. Have mercy on me. Without you I am nothing. Yet you have honoured me and made me the father of your Son. Make me ever watchful for his safety from this day forth.

And while, because you will it, Lord, I may be his father for a while, I know you are his true Father, that you always have been and will be so forever. While I may love and care for him with the help of your grace in these his vulnerable childhood years, I give his whole life to you, and everything to you, my God, because everything comes from you. I bless your Holy Name.

Reflection

We tend to think of Joseph as a father figure—devoted, providing, working and caring. We see him as a model of loving stability. But Joseph has a terrible shock in this story. It reminds us that Joseph's experience was not of unbroken security and confidence. He surely feels ashamed here that he has failed in the one task the Lord has given him—an immense task: nothing less than the upbringing of God's only Son. But notice what Joseph does.

He remains close to and supportive of Mary as they journey through this trial together. And, despite his shame and failure, Joseph turns straight to God in prayer. He admits his fault fully and discovers not just forgiveness, which would be wonderful enough, but the complete resolution of his problem, the restoration of the lost son to his parents, and more. He gains a new understanding of his son's awareness of his relationship to God. He takes a huge step in the deepening surrender of his own life.

We are often reminded that we are all called to be saints. It can seem too daunting an ambition. But the famous saints, like St Joseph, had their own journeys to make, and failures along the way proved no impediment. We don't have to be perfect to be saints. We can be weak; we can be broken. But if we give our weakness to God, like Joseph, and place our lives in his hands, he will live in us and lead us into holiness.

Prayer

Thank you, Lord, for the example of St Joseph. Thank you for his unfailing dedication and love despite the times of fear and difficulty. Thank you for his readiness to pray. Help us, like the Holy Family, to cling to you in moments of trial. May we support each other as these parents did. Help us to pray sincerely, to place our broken selves in your hands and allow you to lead us closer to you. May we, like the young Jesus in this story, seek you in your temple and may we follow Joseph's steps on a path to sainthood. Amen

The Luminous Mysteries

1. The Baptism of Jesus

John the Baptist dedicated his whole life unquestioningly to the mission to which he was appointed: to prepare a way for the Lord. Without luxuries of any kind in his life, he spent day after day preaching a baptism of repentance for sin, preparing his people for a new way of life. He knew his cousin, Jesus, was the Son of God. Knowing this, he didn't expect that Jesus would come to him asking to receive baptism in the waters of the river Jordan. But he must have been waiting for his opportunity to proclaim him the Son of God. The spirit of the Lord was with him, and perhaps through the Holy Spirit he sensed when this event was approaching and realised its significance as it closed.

A Turning Point

Lord God, here I am, on my knees before you once again. But not to beg your forgiveness or to plead for help this time. Things have changed, as you always knew they would. No—I'm here to bless you, and to thank you for this day.

You taught me to expect it. I knew that he would come one day. I have told them over and over that there was one coming after me. One greater than I. One that I have been appointed to announce to this needy, broken world.

What I hadn't expected was your intervention, your power, that mighty revelation of your presence among us. And your love! I praise and thank you, Lord my God, for the wonder of it all.

You showed me, from the early hours of this morning, that this was the day. It throbbed with new life and promise from my first awaking. The sun lit the low clouds with fierce dawn firelight. As the orb freed itself and rose above the cloud, the land sharpened with shadows, and the hills glowed in new colours. My heart had a stronger pulse. I spent those early hours in fervent prayer with you, my God. Had I done the work you gave me? Had I prepared them? Could I be worthy of this meeting?

Later, at the riverside the reeds blew in lovely winding movements as the breeze stirred. I knew the whole place was alive in a new way. Yet nothing was obviously unusual. People were beginning to gather, slowly, as they always did. Little families, twos and threes, a scattered trail of figures strung along the pathway, larger groups, clustering between the reedbeds.

There was no one out of the ordinary. So, I sought to do the work you have always asked of me, to face them with their wickedness and shortcomings. To lead them to repentance. To prepare the way for the Lord.

They gathered more closely near the stretch of bank where I usually baptise the contrite. I spoke, more forcefully I think than ever, because of the imminence of his arrival. "Turn from your sins," I urged them. "Turn, while there is still time. Repent and be baptised for the forgiveness of your wicked deeds." Some came weeping, some pushing and shoving. Others hung back or drew away, uncertain. A young man came declaring his desire to repent. I led him first into the river and my disciples came to guide him and to keep the others back.

The sun was already warm, but the river water grasping our legs was strong and cold. He gasped at the immersion, but his face as he emerged was like an angel. He gave me such thanks, but not in speech. And as he was led away, others came. I knew, Lord God, that you were blessing the work.

I grew utterly absorbed in the task, in the usual rhythms of the day, in speaking, challenging, assuring, watching each face for signs of genuine contrition, knowing from you, Lord my God, what you wished me to do. One man, who came laughing, my disciples led away. I prayed he would come back one day. I watched, again and again, the shock and the expanding joy in eyes emerging through rivulets and drops of river water which caught the sparkle of the sunlight as they fell. Gradually the river water darkened with the stirring of the silt beneath. I looked away down the Jordan's length, at the beauty of this water course which blessed our land. That was when I caught my first glimpse of him.

I thought at first it was the sun that picked him out for me. The white garment shone. He stood at the river's edge some distance away. I faltered in what I was doing. I blinked, wondering if he was real or a vision. Then as I stood looking towards him, he looked up at me. Excitement surged through my heart. The brightness of his figure seemed to generate a glow around him. That was when I realised the light shone out of him. It was not the sun's reflection; it came from him. He was the Son of God. There was a burst of joy inside me. He had come. Truly he had come to me. I think I must have grinned. He gave a gentle smile back and began moving towards me. No one made way for him. He had to wend a way between the crowding people. It struck me as extraordinary. This shining figure moved among them, and they did not see.

At last, I realised that it was only to me that you made him visible, Lord God of Israel. To the people he was hidden. I knew he was the Lamb of God, but they had no idea. So, my task still stood. I was to be his herald, his announcer. I was too awestruck at first to contemplate saying anything at all. In silence, as everyone around waited for my ministering to resume, I simply watched him pick his haphazard course through the people.

He was a grown man now, tall, bearded. I couldn't possibly have recognised him from the dim and distant memories of our childhood meetings. Worlds of change had divided us since then, since those early days when my mother and father were still alive and full of stories of my birth and his birth, and how I had greeted him while still within my mother's womb by leaping for joy in his presence—when he, too, was still within the womb of his mother, Mary from Nazareth. It was the same joy I felt now. It sang in my heart and soul. My father had been full of prophecies of how I would be the herald of his coming. And here he came, closer now, closer to his herald. I must speak, but I could not. My tongue was fast. I gazed at his lithe figure, his youthful face. He was far more boyish still than I.

Briefly the intervening years passed through my mind: my years of resorting to the wild places after my parents died. Escaping the anxious care of neighbours who had undertaken to watch over me. I needed the space and freedom. It was there that God spoke to me, there that the visions of the lost people of Yahweh overwhelmed and fired me. From time to time I ventured back into the village just to show the neighbours that I flourished in my unfettered new existence. I thrived on wild food in the open spaces. Once I had grown to adulthood, they ceased to worry. And people began to visit me, to turn to me, to seek the truth about God.

I could see in his eyes, as he drew close now, a certain mildly amused surprise at my unkempt appearance. I had toughened in these wilderness years. My skin was coarsened and my beard untrimmed. I had aged, but he... His eyes held at once a youthful innocence and a depth of wisdom. He joined the queue meekly, as if he were no different from anybody else. How could they not see that he was of a different order from the rest of us?

A decision simply happened within me. I stepped towards him, holding out a hand.
"This is the Lamb of God," I spoke aloud at last. People turned to look. "This is the Lamb of God I talked to you about. The one who was always destined to come after me, though he ranks before me. He is the Lamb who will take away the sins of the world. I am not worthy..."

I was halfway to my knees, partly out of an instinctive reverence, partly to show them how they all should be reacting, but Jesus raised his hand to stop me. I faltered into silence. His hand took mine and raised me to my feet. We stared, face to face, so close.
"It can't be right," I blurted at last, "for you to come to me for baptism. It is I who need to receive..."

He lifted his hand to my mouth to stop me speaking, then laid the hand on my shoulder and drew me into an embrace. No one had touched me so closely in years and yet it felt as natural as breathing. People were watching open-eyed now. Their talk had faded to whispers and murmuring. They fell back a little in surprise.

"It is fitting that I come to you, my cousin," he stated calmly, withdrawing from the warm embrace we had shared. "I want to be baptised, by you, in the Jordan waters."

"But you," I protested still. "You do not need… You are the Son…"

"To fulfil all righteousness," he said. "I must be one with all the people."

As we drew apart, we shared a long and level gaze of new understanding. This was God's plan, not of our devising. I gave way.

"Then come forward," I invited him. "Turn afresh to God and let us enter the water."

My cousin shed his outer cloak and sandals and arranged them in a neat pile beside a stone. As we waded the few strides that took us beyond the shallows, the crowd was quieted. I had no need to make the usual insistent demand for a renunciation of sinfulness. It was suddenly very simple. No sound but the plash and surge of water as our steps plunged deeper. No words as he allowed my disciples to hold his arms and support his shoulders as they dipped him backwards gently, slowly, into the cold, dark body of the Jordan water. I leaned forward to raise him out. His eyes were closed; water streamed from his hair.

There was always the huge wash of sound as water cascaded back down through clothing to its river level. But this sound was deeper, strange. I heard a murmur in the crowd and glanced round, catching sight of startled expressions, wide eyes directed upwards. There was another burst of sound, a gentle thunder. As I looked up, a brilliant light began to pierce the skies.

Like an earthquake it broke within me—utter conviction that this was your act, my God. You wanted to be in this moment as in no other. Not just as the hidden voice within our hearts or in the scriptures, but in immediacy—I knew not how. My blood was racing already; my mind blanked with awe. The light had spread now; it was steady, and it transformed the landscape, eliminating the sun's pale shadows. Slowly from within its heart in the height of heaven emerged a white, blazing shape. It descended towards us and began to swoop from side to side as it came steadily lower. It seemed like clustered flames at first, like a white fire, but it grew slowly clearer until we saw a white bird, like a dove. I knew this was the Holy Spirit. I held my breath in amazement. As it came lower still, the dove circled a little while, swooping over the river, the crowds, the reedbeds, wings outstretched, before it settled and hovered directly above the head of my cousin, Jesus. There was a long moment of intense silence. My God, my God, I breathed, without a sound escaping my lips. Thank you for your presence. Thank you for this gift of the Holy Spirit. Praise you. I have baptised my cousin with water, like everyone, but You are baptising him with the Holy Spirit. Jesus was receiving a baptism greater and deeper and more wonderful than any I could have offered.

When I looked round, I saw there was no need to struggle to find a voice in order to explain to the people. They were on their knees. They knew this was God's work. There was a total silence; even babies were hushed. Then that thunder from heaven gave a warning, and a deep, powerful voice sounded from the skies.

"This is my Son, the Beloved, in whom I am well pleased."

My God, your voice filled the skies and resonated across the whole open scene. It filled my ears, and I could take in nothing else. I think my other senses died momentarily; I was just lost in your voice. Only aware of You. Your words repeated themselves somewhere within me. And although they had been so loud that all could hear, they were not frightening. There was no harshness in their tone. There was love.

I turned to Jesus. He stood, eyes closed, in the full glare of the light which streamed from heaven, the Holy Spirit hovering above him, the sound of his Father's voice still hanging in the air around us. God's beloved. It was the love in that majestic voice that became more and more vivid to me. When my cousin finally raised his eyes to mine, I could see love in them. He was beloved of God, and he loved his Father deeply in return. It was so new to me. I was awed. I was unsure what to do now. I praised the Lord aloud, over and over.

As the light began to fade and a faint murmuring was beginning among the people, I realised that Jesus was wading out of the water. I turned to follow. He picked his way, holding his clothing to hinder its sticking to his limbs. My disciples were gathering around the shore, anxious to speak of what had happened. Before I had realised, my cousin had already picked up his clothes and was merging into the crowd. I would have followed, drawn to him irresistibly, but for the eagerness of my disciples. My heart was singing at this glorious confirmation of what my mother had always told me. That he was the Son of God—and our Messiah. The chosen one. The beloved.

You held me there with my followers, I know that now, Lord. I could not go with him. He is destined for a new life, lived in a new way. I must fade now. This is a turning point. I must announce him still to others, speak about him. But I must grow smaller now, as he grows greater. He is the Son of God, whom I have been blessed to serve.

Blessed are you Lord, in love and in power. I praise you and thank you for the privilege of having lived this day. Thank you, almighty God. Praise and bless you for ever.

Reflection

This first Luminous Mystery recalls an astonishing and multifaceted event. A reunion of cousins who had recognised each other in a mysterious way before they were even born. A seeking of baptism by the very Son of God from a mere mortal being. The fulfilment of John the Baptist's calling to be a herald of the Lord. And more still than all this—the manifestation of the nature of the Trinity. The powerful voice of God the Father declaring his love to his Son, Jesus, in the visible presence of the Holy Spirit.

The story in this Mystery proved a turning point in the life of John the Baptist, because he recognised that his role was fulfilled, and this was why he declared that he himself must grow smaller while Jesus grew greater. He gave way to his cousin, the Lamb of God. Yet this is more than a changing of roles; it marks a change in the nature of baptism. John's baptism in water for repentance of sins is transformed into Christ's baptism in the Holy Spirit—and this in its turn affects each one of us. We receive that same baptism when we receive the sacrament. It is marked or symbolised by water, but it is the work of the Holy Spirit who comes to dwell in us.

Prayer

Loving God, may we imitate all those present at this scene in marvelling at the revelation of the Trinity. May we never cease to venerate the majesty, glory and mystery of the Father, Son and Holy Spirit. We thank you for the wondrous gift of baptism. We praise you for the Holy Spirit's coming into our lives. Holy Spirit, make us always aware of your silent but powerful presence and grant us the fullness of all the gifts which flow from you. Amen

2. The Wedding Feast of Cana

"This was the first of the signs given by Jesus," wrote John, in his Gospel, of this well-known story. Jesus effectively rescues the hosts and their servants from the shame and disaster of running out of wine halfway through a wedding feast—a public occasion. It is a great story, with suspense, panic, mystery and a happy ending. Its position as the very first "sign" given by our Lord at the beginning of his ministry, gives it prominence. Why does it have such importance? Let us relive the story first. Let us follow it through the eyes of one who was there. One who was in a situation that gave him a close-up view of all that happened.

Crisis Averted

The room was warm and rang with laughter. They were a beautiful couple. It had been a joyful wedding ceremony, and up to now the feast had been magnificent. I couldn't help thinking what a shame it was for this disaster to befall them, though I ought to have been thinking of our own skins. What would happen when we told the chief steward that we had managed somehow to run out of wine? The joy in people's faces would change; in some to disappointment, in some to embarrassment, or shame, or perhaps sheer rage. All our jobs could be on the line. For there was no way out; we had searched everywhere.

"Go on, Amos," the others were urging me. "Someone's got to tell him."

I could have answered, "why me?" but I shrugged instead. I had been there longer than any of them. I had fewer dependants—and broad shoulders. I could take the steward's anger. Nothing could shock me anymore. So, I went through the nearest arched doorway back into the hall and managed all too quickly to catch the steward's eye. He swept across the cluttered space between us with all the grandeur and presence of his station. One of the ladies on a nearby table looked up, noticing his swift movement.

"What is it?" he asked in a fierce whisper, adding, when I hesitated, "Well?"

"Sir, we have run out of wine."

He pushed past me, striding into the cool, stone corridor where the others were clustered. I followed in his wake.

"What's this you say, run out of wine?" He turned back to me. "Impossible. Find some, find some."

"We've looked everywhere…" I blurted, but to no avail.

"Well look again."

"We have, sir, it's no good," offered young Tobias, trying to help.

"You're quite right, it's no good!" The chief steward rounded on poor Tobias. "No good at all!"

"No, sir," said the lad, crestfallen.

"Well, get out and find some elsewhere then. Try the big houses. Beg, borrow or steal. But get on with it!" He turned away, stiff-faced. "Go to the vineyard if you have to. I'll settle up with them later."

"But the vineyard's a day's journey…" Silas' protest went unheard.

I spread my arms; hands opened upwards. "Well perhaps two of us had better…"

Tobias dug me in the ribs, and I broke off, turning to him. The direction of his startled gaze guided mine back towards the doorway to the banquet hall. A lady stood there silently, observing us, with a knowing smile on her features. She was the one who had noticed the steward's extreme haste. We were silenced too. Then a young man came up beside her, darker haired, but like her—probably her son. She gave him the briefest glance.

"Do whatever he tells you," she said to us.

As we stood dumbfounded, the young man stepped out into the corridor, looked about him and spotted the water jars for ablutions lined up against the stone wall in semi-darkness. Pointing at them, he told us to fill them with water.

What there was of common sense in me tried to rise in protest. How was this going to help? Why should we listen? He was just an ordinary man. But something else silenced me. What it was I don't know, but not one of us voiced objections to this pointless exercise. No, we all set to, carrying water to the jars in bowls and buckets, hoisting and pouring, slopping some on the flags in our confusion. We filled every last one of the six enormous jars to the brim before he told us to stop.

"Now draw some off into a jug," he said, very calmly.

We gazed at one another for a moment, but still no one spoke. My common sense had fled before something within this man. Not power, exactly. He was not commanding, or masterful. It was something quiet, unearthly.

"Go on," I said to Tobias, handing him a jug.

With his habitually innocent expression, young Tobias bent to the spigot of the nearest water jar, lifted it, and let the water run into the jug.

"Now take it to the chief steward," the man said.

Tobias looked up at me for a moment, but I just nodded and let him go. It would bring catastrophe, but what could I do? It was beyond me now. We watched Tobias make his way into the hall, and then through the crowded tables to where the steward was wielding large platters of food. We saw the steward set these down and lift a fresh cup to the jug Tobias proffered. I waited for the explosion of his fury when he saw exactly what Tobias was pouring out. I closed my eyes.

There were no raised voices, much to my surprise, but above the hubbub of general conversation I began to discern the voice of the chief steward and it seemed suffused with cheerfulness.

"It's good wine!" cried Silas, who had listened better than I. "It's wine! Get some more, boys. Take the jugs round."

"Wine?" said I. "How could...?" I turned towards the stranger, the young man, who had wrought this miracle. But he had already turned away and was helping his mother back into the seat she had occupied before at the table. I felt I should be thanking him, but there was such excitement among all the serving men, that they were in danger of falling over one another in their rush to fill jugs from the water jars.

"Careful!" I shouted. "Watch what you're doing!"

When they had all disappeared into the hall, I went myself to the second water jar, and took its contents into a jug of my own. I couldn't tell in the darkness what the contents were, but I followed the others, and began to refill folks' empty cups. It poured out, gleaming and a deep ruby red. I was shaken to the roots. The jug shook in my hand. I couldn't believe this was happening. And I had thought nothing could shock me!

"This is the best wine yet!" A loud voice reached my ears from the high table. "The very best! Most people serve the best sort first, but you've done the opposite. You've saved the most sublime till now!!"

The best wine—sublime! My heart beat fast. I spotted the tousled head of Tobias, over at the other side of the hall; the chief steward had approached him and laid a hand on the lad's shoulder. I didn't hear his words, but I didn't need to. I saw the grins on their faces. I steadied myself on a nearby serving table, and let joy begin to temper this headiness I felt. What a change of fortunes. What a miracle! And who on earth was this young man who had saved us from catastrophe? I had to know more.

I turned and began to make my way towards him, but I had hardly moved before he spotted my approach. His eyes were friendly, but he raised a finger to his lips, and I hesitated. So, it was to be our secret. Fair enough, I thought, if that's how he wants it. When I reached the table, he had turned away. So, I checked their drinking cups, filled up one that was empty and turned away without a word.

I could keep a secret. Yet it always puzzled me, why a man would choose to share a secret with the servants and keep it from his host and all the important guests.

Reflection

The miracle performed in this story, the second Mystery of Light, though wonderful, is hardly earth-shattering: not like the later miracles of Jesus, such as the raising of Lazarus from the tomb. It solves an immediate crisis and enables people to enjoy themselves. So, was it placed first because, like so many really big things, Jesus' ministry started small? Or does John's word "sign" point to greater meaning?

A wedding feast is a frequent biblical image of God's relationship with his people. All through the Old Testament, God woos Israel, wanting their response of love. But His people, though enthusiastic at times, often allowed their loyalty to run out, like the wine. Perhaps, in the story, the supply of new wine for the wedding feast should remind us of the miraculous provision God made for us, when He sent His own Son to rescue His damaged and straying people. Jesus saves the day in Cana with the pouring out of wine. It surely foreshadows the day when he saves Israel and all peoples by pouring out his blood on the Cross.

Jesus could not have come to Earth without Mary; so maybe it's no accident that this prior miracle is prompted by Mary's observation and guidance of the servants. Though pregnant with significance, however, this event is not even made known to the guests at the feast. Jesus prevents Amos in this story from spreading the news. Yet all the servants know. Is this, too, a "sign" of Jesus' special love for the poor?

Prayer

Jesus, help us to learn to emulate the servants in obeying Mary's instructions. Help us to give the poor special love and attention as you did. We run out of love, Lord. We are nothing without you. Make us realise that our own resources are woefully inadequate; we need to trust in your power. May we thus, like the wedding guests, come to drink, not the water of worldly life, but the rich wine of your Kingdom. Thank you for your mighty love which brings this new gift of fullness of life. Amen

3. The Proclamation of The Kingdom

Jesus came among us to proclaim that the Kingdom of God is close at hand. He spoke to people, teaching them, often through parables; he healed the sick, the lame, the deaf and blind; he drove out demons; he calmed the sea and multiplied the loaves and fishes to feed a vast multitude. He gave us beautiful words about forgiveness and love. He came to restore what was lost, to retrieve the Kingdom of his Father, as it would have been without mankind's falling into sin. He was renewing the fullness of creation. He brought us new life. This story is just one remarkable and dramatic example of restoration.

New Life

I still saw the clustered women below me, even though we were outside now and out of that fetid sick room, that narrow house. They led the ragged procession as it moved slowly up the curving road and then through the opening in the old stone walls. In the sunlight, the shadows were clearer to me than the little figures. A pattern of shapes crossed the wide tract of parched land towards the burial ground where they would lay what remained of me in the earth.

It was from a height I looked down now. Yet I could clearly see the bier as it was carried along, and on it, the rigid shape of the body within which I used to live. I felt no sadness at being so detached from it. Just this sense of space, of being endless. From within this peace, I could survey the whole scene: the low buildings of Nain; the distant hills; the long road through the rocky landscape; even some distant figures on the road, a crowd of them, making their way towards the city.

It was only the shrill cries of the women that broke through the peace enwrapping me and brought me stabs of pain. I could tell my mother's voice among the others. Only for her I fought against the intoxication of this enfolding calm. She had no one but me. She had the neighbours for now, of course, and a crowd of city folk. They came to mourn. It was traditional. But afterwards she would be bereft, both of family and of the means to get by. She would be totally alone—and soon destitute.

The keening of the women seemed to rise to me like gleaming strings, the only frail attachment left between us. I wished they were strong as ropes, and that they could haul me down to Earth. But back in that familiar, clammy, darkened room, over the last few days, fever and pain had drained my body of its life. There could be no return. The thought struck me with new impact, a great boulder of grief, and unbalanced things. The peace which carried me seemed to twist and slacken in a sickening lurch.

When I recovered, I was nearer to them than before. I saw my mother looking upward to the sky as she paced on with slow, unsteady steps. I knew she was appealing to heaven. Dear God, I thought, if only heaven would send her help! But who was there? She lowered her careworn face at last and I watched her narrow her eyes against the distant light. She pulled her black shawl tighter around her head and narrow shoulders. I followed her gaze and realised that she had spotted the approaching group of travellers. They were getting close— one man ahead of all the others. As I watched, he changed the direction of his walk, moving now not towards the city gate, but curving sideways, making towards my mother. But he was just a weary, dust-streaked traveller. Sympathetic to my mother maybe, but not the answer to her prayer.

Faintly I heard the talk that passed between them as he turned and began to walk beside her. It was strangely muffled; I couldn't distinguish words. As I watched, this man stepped forward from my mother's side towards the bier that she followed. As he touched it, the bearers halted and I saw others in his band stop and gather around him, at a respectful distance. There were more, still approaching up the road. Was he a leader of some kind? A priest?

Although a total stranger, he seemed to lift his hand towards my lifeless remains. I had this fleeting thought that it might be some kind of blessing; and then the whole picture was obliterated, the peace around me fractured. Is this death? The flash of this question was the last thing I remember before I lost myself completely. There was just whiteness, an explosion of light. I have no idea for how long.

The first thing I became aware of after this was the sensation of something gently touching my hand. Warm fingers laid over mine. As the shock of this realisation struck home in me, something pulsed in my heart, and I felt the gasp of air rush into my lungs. I felt the warmth of that hand's touch travel up my arm. It spread through me. What was this? I tried to open my eyes, but there was only a swimming of light at first.

"Young man," I heard his voice. Rich tones, almost inside me and not like the muffled voices earlier. "Get up. Arise, I tell you."

As the world around me became clearer, I found strength returning to my limbs. I grasped the sides of the bier, pushed myself up. I saw him now with my human, living eyes so vividly before me. Just a traveller, bedraggled, dark hair blown dusty in the desert wind, creases in his face. But that face! Majestic. Such power in his eyes. What could I say?

"Who… I thank… my Lord… how…" Words tumbled out of me; I couldn't get them straight. Who was he?

A smile grew across his features. My mother came up close. He lifted up my hand and placed it into hers. There were tears pouring down her face, and I felt the pricking warmth of my responding tears as I struggled from the bier onto uncertain legs and fell into her embrace.

"A miracle," someone shouted in the crowd.

But the man, prophet, teacher, priest, whoever he was, turned away meekly, as if it were nothing out of the ordinary. He would have walked on calmly towards the old city gateway, had not the crowd grown thicker, jostled close and barred his way.

As my mother and I pulled out of the first hug of our reunion, and gazed on one another's joy-filled faces, we heard the voices all around us.
"A great prophet has appeared among us!"
"God has come to save his people!"

It took a while before he persuaded the crowd to disperse; but the wonder of that miracle has stayed with us much longer. We marvel each and every day at what he has done for us. Neither of us, even now, can quite believe it has happened. And why us? He didn't even know who we were. Perhaps there is some truth in what mother said one day.

"I saw the look in his eyes," she murmured thoughtfully, gazing into mine. "He has a mother of his own."

Reflection

The widow in this story, who is never named, is becoming destitute. With the death of her son, she has nothing. No family, no money, no life. But the touch of Jesus transforms things. He brings her son literally from death to life. He brings back to her not only the family she needs and the means to live— and the reason to live—but also new gifts of wonder and joy. She weeps tears of happiness, and her son joins her in them. Their relationship is restored. The people are carried away with amazement at the actions of this "prophet". Everything is changed.

This is the miracle of the touch of Jesus. It was literally the physical touch of the incarnate Christ, of course, bringing life in the story. But Jesus lives still and longs to touch our lives in so many ways, through the Holy Spirit, through the words of scripture, through his real presence in the Eucharist. Think about his transforming power. Think how you could reach out to his touch in your own life. The Kingdom of God is close at hand.

Prayer

Dear Jesus, you came into this world to touch our lives, to change us, to bring us out of the darkness of sin and death into the light of love. Thank you, Jesus. May we be transformed by your gentle touch, as were this mother and son. Help us to repent and turn to you. Come into our hearts and take control of our lives. We want to live in the Kingdom of God, to come to life in its fullness, just as you promised. May we obtain the gifts and graces, the understanding, love and joy we need to draw others into your Kingdom too. Amen

4. The Transfiguration

Most of the people Jesus met in his lifetime on Earth assumed he was human and normal ("the carpenter's son, surely"), like everybody else. Obviously, he looked simply human. Some knew otherwise, of course, like his mother and father, from the beginning. Others realised, like Simeon and Anna, and more gradually the apostles. Lots of people sensed something different about him, like those who witnessed the raising of the son of the widow of Nain from the bier that was carrying him to his grave.

This is the story of the one unique occasion when Jesus took on a different appearance. Seeing this was only granted to three of his disciples. One of them tells the story.

Mount Tabor

The day we climbed Mount Tabor is one of my most treasured memories. I remember it all the more clearly because Jesus told us to speak of it to no one. I so badly wanted to spread the news of the realisation that had overwhelmed me. But he was adamant.

"Tell no one," he said. "Tell no one about the vision until the Son of Man has risen from the dead."

We didn't know what he meant about the Son of Man rising from the dead; nor did we understand why it was so important to keep silent. But we had learnt to obey. Neither James, nor Peter, nor I myself ever spoke of it in the succeeding weeks. But we remembered.

It was all deeply etched in my mind. I went over and over it every time we lay down to sleep, in those quiet moments before weariness overtook me. I loved those times. They gave me a space in which the memories could burn in my heart. And they did, truly.

It had begun ordinarily enough. Jesus wanted to take us to a quiet place to pray. It was a habit with which we had all now grown familiar. It was often a hillside he chose: some steep, deserted bank, beneath a scattering of trees, perhaps, or beside a narrow mountain stream. Often it did not remain deserted, of course. People followed him everywhere. Several times his quest for quietude turned into another public carnival of teaching and healing. Perhaps that was why he chose Mount Tabor. It was the biggest, steepest and least accessible mountain in the area.

It was a tough climb on a hot day, even for fit men. Maybe since we left the boats and the lives of fishermen, exchanging them for this strange, nomadic existence, our muscles had weakened. Certainly, our breath came hard, and the effort seemed a prolonged one. Yet Jesus led us on, higher and higher up the rocky half-defined pathways created by goats, probably, rather than by men. When, eventually, we reached the summit, we felt we had almost climbed into the sky. From here we could look down on the wide, level valley of Jezreel that stretched beneath us, its plots and varying crop patterns tiny at the vast distance that our climb had opened up beneath us.

Jesus urged us back from the vantage point from which the valley could be seen. He led us up a gentle rise towards a group of trees. We followed mutely, expecting him to find a place to settle for an extended time of quiet prayer. I loved these times too. To be with him anywhere was wonderful, but to share in the same peaceful silence, with a mild breeze and occasional birdsong the only interruptions was particularly blessed. But this time, before he had even reached a shady place to settle, something quite amazing happened. His whole figure, before us, seemed to begin to glow as if in a concentrated beam of light. We looked about, but this strange light had no visible source; we quickly realised that it must come from him. And it intensified, rapidly, even as we watched. His garments turned white suddenly—brilliant, brilliant white—shining with a whiter light than any of us had ever seen or could have imagined. As he turned to us, his face shone like the blaze of the sun.

We stopped in our tracks. I held my breath. What was this? I felt a need to shade my eyes, the light was so piercingly strong, and yet I could not take my eyes away. Let them burn. This was no normal worldly experience. It caught my heart. He was transformed. An unearthly light, like silver fire, radiated from him. He was ennobled; he was magnificent. And we men stood before him dumbfounded.

Should we worship him, praise him, raise him up in our arms? Or fall prostrate at his feet? This astounding spectacle seemed to demand a response, but we were dumb, and rooted to the ground. And even as we marvelled at his transformation, other things happened to make this day even stranger. On either side of him, in other pools of light, two shapes were slowly materialising, two figures, men. They seemed to be in a conversation with our Lord, but the voices were indistinct. As their forms clarified, they became identifiable to anyone who knew the Holy Scriptures. One was Moses carrying the two stone tablets he had been given on a different mountain, and the other was Elijah, his cloak billowing and a hint of fire glowing from the palms of his hands, upheld as if in prayer.

Peter spoke suddenly. He had the same urge as I had, to make some response, only he had the impetuosity to act on it. I stood by, open-mouthed.

"Lord," gasped Peter, "it is wonderful for us to be here. If you wish, I will make three tents here, one for you, one for Moses and one for Elijah. If you think…"

There he stopped, suddenly aware, like James and me, of a darkness that had rapidly swept onto and now shrouded us in deep shade. I dropped to my knees. This was beyond us. I was overwhelmed. What was happening? I looked up into the sky. The sun had been totally obscured by a dark but bright-edged cloud, and even as I gazed up into it, a huge voice seemed to emanate from its depths. The others collapsed to their knees on either side of me. I think the violent pang of fear which ran through my heart ran through theirs as well.

"This is my Son," announced a deep and sonorous voice from above, "the Beloved. He enjoys my favour. Listen to him."

I shook; I quaked. Maybe it was the whole mountain that trembled. I had never heard such a voice or felt such awe. But the words spoken sank into my mind. They seemed to carve themselves deeply into my soul. They were all that existed in those moments. "This is my Son, the Beloved. Listen to him."

We had heard the voice of God Himself. Nothing else was possible. My mind whirled. Almighty God had spoken. He had spoken to us and declared to us that Jesus was His Son. So, it was true. The words were like a song in my heart. It was true; all true! It was not simply that the light of heaven had shone upon him. It was within him. He was of God. We had seen him in his true nature.

Jesus was the beloved Son of God! He was here with us, a man, and he was divine! And we were to listen to him. I vowed I would listen to him always.

My fear had already changed into wonder, excitement, and a sort of abandonment. He was divine! Nothing else mattered. From the glorious, shining figure of Jesus, I turned to my brother to share the wonder. But his face was ashen. I put my arm around his shoulders, and he clung to me. He was my elder brother, but he seemed to shake with terror and not see what this must mean.

I held him close, to try to quell the trembling of his big frame, laying my head on his shoulder, so that my eyes were hidden in his hair and I could no longer see what was happening. But only the briefest moment passed before there was a touch, a gentle touch on my own shoulder. I knew it was the hand of Jesus. We broke apart and I looked about me. Sunlight was everywhere again, the cloud evaporated. Jesus was as he always was, his robe its usual colour, his face shadowed. He was leaning over Peter now. It was as if that flaring silver light in him had never been.

"Stand up," Jesus said. "Do not be afraid."

The other two staggered to their feet. There was relief on their features, that Jesus had become his normal self again. But I gazed at him from my knees, still astounded. He was the Son of God. I had to kneel before him. He was divine! He had told us this before, of course. Peter had declared it and I had believed. Or so I had thought. Certainly, I had loved him; I had hoped in this strangely powerful man. But now everything was changed for me. He was the Son of God. God loved him. I would never, ever doubt again. He was my Lord, to my dying day.

Jesus held out his hand to me, and helped me to rise. His eyes told me that he knew what had happened to me.

"My dear John," he said. "Come, stand. You cannot spend all day on your knees. We have to go back down the mountain." Then he added, "You will not forget this day. But you must speak of it to no one."

"No one at all?" I questioned, as we began to make our way back down the rocky pathways of Mount Tabor.

"No one," he said, reiterating his demand, so that the others heard as well.

"If that's what you really want," said James.

"It's my command," Jesus answered, stopping in his downhill progress and turning back to us, to emphasise his point. "Tell no one about the vision until the Son of Man has risen from the dead."

Reflection

Just imagine witnessing, with your own dazzled eyes, the vision of Christ transformed, the power of the full light of divinity. It must have been difficult for the disciples to hold their tongues. But the real effect of this experience was indelibly and lastingly written in their hearts. It surely deepened their awe, banished any lingering doubts, confirmed them in faith, and opened them to his love. In this story, it certainly filled John with reverence, awe and profound humility. He knew a deeper level of worship; he resolved to listen always.

Awe and reverence are in short supply in our society. There is fame; there is notoriety; but little deep respect for authority. Awe before the divine seems almost lost, but fortunately not quite. Most people retain a sense of wonder before some things. It might be the beauty of mountains or flowers, or the power in music. Their reaction to these things is perhaps a sign of their deeper but unrecognised yearning for God.

At the end of this story, however, the disciples had to descend from the mountain and return to normal life, keeping this treasured experience hidden, at least for a time. This is a foretaste and perhaps a promise, but meanwhile they have more to do in their usual world.

Prayer

Lord, you gave the three chosen disciples the amazing gift of a direct revelation of the divine light of your true being. Help all people to discern, through the Church and through the world, the hand of God in all creation. May we all follow the disciples in discovering the reverence and worship we owe to you. Open our hearts in true humility and surrender before your goodness. Help us always to remember to listen to you. Strengthen us too, Lord, so that even when we feel far from your light, in the ordinary events of life, down at the bottom of the mountain, we may still cling to and trust in you. Amen

5. The Institution of The Eucharist

This final Luminous Mystery of the Rosary holds an event which is far more than just a story. It is the Last Supper of Christ, his last meal on Earth, and the origin of the Eucharist, the source and summit of our faith, the event which changed history and has been and is recreated at every Mass throughout the world. It is huge. It has foreshadowings and repercussions beyond count. It is hard to do it justice in the confines of a short story. So this story approaches it through eyes that fail to see its whole significance. Yet these eyes belong to someone whose decisions and actions were vital to the working of God's plan.

Outsider

Jesus gets down on his knees and washes our feet. Every one of us. Really. Washes our feet! There we are in this big upper room—grand, stone pillars along its length, fine vaulted ceiling—with the tables all ready, prepared for the feast of the Passover, food and servants waiting, and he starts washing our feet. And when he's finished, he tells us that this is what we have to do for one another. Serve, he means. Lower ourselves to behave like servants. I ask you.

Well, it did for me. I might have been only half-hearted before, in the thoughts that kept straying across my mind, but this settled it once and for all. As I watched him, with the towel round his waist, rubbing one of Thomas's feet, the lingering doubts cleared like birds from carrion when the jackal comes close. I didn't follow him to be a slave. We all thought he was bringing us the promise of a new kingdom; a victory; a better life. A triumph for the people; an end to Roman occupation. Peace and glory. And now he keeps coming up with this weird talk of how he is to be handed over to suffer and to die.

Well, if that's what he wants, some of us aren't above obliging him. Very nice offer I had a while back, from the officers of the guard, and the synagogue officials who hide behind them. Wasn't sure then of course. Told them I'd sleep on it. There was still something about him that made me hesitate. Something powerful in him, I used to think. But now. Well. Their offer would make me quite a wealthy man. Better than a slave. 'Why not?' I say.

As we gather finally around that table, I secretly resolve to agree their price. Then I'll tip them off when I get the chance. I look at him, sitting there, the towel gone now, the centre of attention. He has no idea. All unsuspecting. And it's going to be so easy. Just give them a secret signal, that's all. They'll do the rest. And I'll get the money. Simple. What's to lose?

But meanwhile, I sit here, still acting like one of them. Sharing in wine, food and fellowship. Nothing wrong with that; I can go along with it. That's been the good part all along, come to think of it. Whereas all the wandering about, going from village to village, never knowing where we were going to end up, that was a different story. Cold, wet, exhausted, hungry sometimes—it was never really for me. And curing so many people, whether they deserved it or not. I don't know how the others could go along with it so easily and so long. They loved it, obviously. They're besotted with him.

Look at John, now, gazing with those adoring eyes. And Peter and his brother, big stout chaps. Used to be so down-to-earth, good for a laugh, and now something's gone out of them. Look at them, gazing on, dead serious, these pious expressions on their faces, while Jesus blesses the bread and breaks the loaves, as if it's something significant. Then at last the bread gets passed around the table. It's only bread for God's sake. I take my share. I deserve it, don't I? I've followed him for weeks, years. Day after day. And exactly where has it got me? No, I've had my fill of this.

He's blessing the wine now and indulging in more of these raving idiocies he keeps coming up with, about his body and blood. And a new covenant. None of them see through him. A covenant in bread and wine? He's no Messiah, after all, I'm convinced. He's seriously deluded, and possibly dangerous. But I take the wine passed to me. I drink a good draught and smile. Then I call for the bread, but no one seems to hear. They are hanging on his words. I just catch the end of what he is saying:

"One of you will betray me." There is consternation among them at these words; they look at one another, aghast. I confess there is a flutter at my heart, but I give no sign. I look around the others, like one of the crowd. Meanwhile Peter has nudged John, who is closest to Jesus, prompting him to ask who it is who will betray him. John obeys, of course.

"Who is it, Lord?" His voice is a confidential whisper.

"It is the one," replies Jesus, in equally subdued tones (but I catch every word), "to whom I give the piece of bread that I shall dip in the dish."

And he dips this piece of bread in the saltwater and bitter herbs and passes it to me. I keep a straight face and take it from him. To object would attract attention I can do without; this way I can pass it off as meaningless, afterwards, as part of his crazed behaviour. But the pounding of my heart is making that straight face hard to maintain. I bite into the bread. And then he whispers to me.

"What you are going to do, do quickly."

I stop chewing, momentarily. When I resume, the bread sticks on my tongue. I struggle to get it down my throat.

So he knows.

I have feared nothing before this. Yet now, I cannot raise my eyes to his. He knows. And suddenly it commits me more than ever. He is dangerous to me now. I will do the deed. I will see him brought to an end. It's the only way now I will be safe.

So, meek as John, I obey.

I get to my feet, leave the table, and head for the doorway at the end of the room and the stone steps down to the street. I make my way down them into the dark. I look at no one.

I am on my own now.

Reflection

This must be one of the most dramatic moments in the whole of scripture. Judas sets out on his dastardly course of betrayal of the Lord, just at the moment when Jesus is announcing and enacting his amazing gift of the Eucharist to humanity for all ages to come. He is leaving us a legacy, not of money or precious heritage, but of his very being. He leaves us his body and blood—the flesh of his indivisible divine and human self—as food for us to eat as a communion with him, so that he can truly live in us. It is a gift beyond words to express. Perhaps none of us ever fully comprehend it. And yet Judas is unimpressed.

Although he once thought there was some power in Jesus, some hope of a better future, he decides here and now that he has been deluded. He is like Herod meeting John the Baptist in that he is drawn to him, but in the end brings about his death. Herod does it to preserve his reputation in front of his court. Judas does it in revulsion against the idea of service, and in favour of improving his own social ranking and personal pleasure. He is guided by the standards of the world.

Maybe we despise him as a traitor. We should not forget, though, that the world has a hold on us too. Do we not sometimes care more about pleasing other people than pleasing our Lord? Do we refrain from speaking of God, for fear of what others would say? Do we do good things in order to obtain human approval, rather than for their own sakes? Do we leave God out of our lives for a while and indulge in laziness, or gossip, or excessive eating or drinking, because everyone else does it? Of course we do. We are human, and we are sinners. We are entrammelled in the ways of the world.

Prayer

Father, we pray that your eleven faithful disciples may be our model, and not Judas! May we follow them in their growing trust and in their receiving from your table. May we always be grateful for the legacy, the living presence of your Son Jesus in the Eucharist, which he chose to leave for us. We are sorry for all the times we have conformed to worldly standards or sought human approval, rather than yours. Forgive us, Jesus, for we do not deserve even to sit close to you, much less receive your Body and Blood in a miraculous communion with you. Dear Father, you sent your Son into the world not to condemn the world but to save it. Your grace restores us. Thank you for your endless mercy. Amen

The Sorrowful Mysteries

1. The Agony in The Garden

This First Sorrowful Mystery changes the tone. Its name, or just the very word "Agony", lurches us from the years of Jesus' ministry to those of his passion. This is the beginning of the suffering that Jesus chose to undergo, to counter the disobedience and betrayal of Satan and the consequent sinfulness of humankind. It is about obedience and its costs. It is Jesus' "yes" to his Father. It is a dark echo of his mother's "fiat" over three decades before, and it is deeply challenging.

Jesus is alone when this happens. His only human companions fall asleep. Almost every other Mystery of the Rosary has human witnesses, through whose eyes we can imagine the story. But the only witness to Jesus' agony in the garden is the garden itself, the landscape and the trees.

The Mount of Olives

We are old. We are gnarled, grey, twisted, ancient trees. We have thrust out new branches, unfolded fresh leaves and produced our crop of olives, year on year, decade on decade, century on century. We still stand, guardians, watchers in this garden of Gethsemane.

You, our visitors, pilgrims to this place, gaze at us for a few fleeting moments of your fleeting lives. You gaze with some respect, which pleases us. Some of you know what Gethsemane means. Many of you try to imagine what it was like here over two thousand years ago, when this garden spread its boundaries more widely, when we were a little less gnarled and aged, when the big church had not been built and our rocky terrain lay open to the skies. Some of you catch a glimpse of the visit of the Son of God in your souls' imagination.

But we remember. To our roots, we remember. It is bound in our ancient wood forever. Like the scar of an ancient and penetrating wound. And it was like a wounding. It hurt to see how the Lord suffered.

He came in the dwindling light of early evening, humbly clothed, unremarkable, with just a handful of companions. We heard them speaking in subdued voices, and then watched as his disciples settled themselves to wait, finding some physical support for their tired bodies against the trunk of one our number, or against a well-placed outcrop of stone. Jesus meanwhile moved slowly, up the gradual slope, treading a lonely path into our shelter and our scattered shade, till finally he sank to his knees on a dry, rocky patch in our midst. We arched our branches close to him, listening, as he called on his Father.

They spoke together there, Father and Son. It was silent. There was no sound from them. Yet we heard his pleading clearly. We felt how fiercely his strong, earthly, fully human nature longed to cling to the lovely joys of life on Earth: to friends, to fellowship, to all the wondrous senses of the human frame. The sight of faces, figures, landscapes, the touch of hands, the smells of fire and food, the sounds of lapping water at the lakeside, of birds unseen within the clustered leaves of trees. These he loved, these he craved to keep, and yet he heard the call of his Father to lay down this precious gift of life on earth so that many, many countless thousands more human souls could live in full and right relationship with their source of life, with their Creator. So that they could live untrammelled, unbetrayed by their dark enemy who lurked in every corner of their lives: a threat to all who lived on Earth, now and for numberless years into the future, unless his powers could be staunched, his strong wings clipped, by a human soul big enough and loving enough to burden itself with all the evil fruits of his treachery and take this sinfulness into a sacrifice of death.

He stumbled to his feet abruptly, the discord within him irreconcilable. He returned to his disciples, but before he even reached them, knew he must obey. So, after murmured indignation at their falling into sleep and a plea for their prayers (not for himself, but for their own salvation), he came back to his Father, here among us.

We remember. How could we not remember? The ground trembled. It was the moment the world changed. He pleaded; oh, how desperately he pleaded for this cup of death to pass him by. Yet even as he pleaded, he knew it was the summit of his whole mission, and the dearest purpose of his Father. As he fell, full-length upon the rock, his arms extended, we heard his wordless prayer for the desire and for the will to be obedient. Yet the thought of bearing the burden of the sins of all the world overwhelmed him.

Again, he rose to his feet, turned, traversed our uneven ground towards his companions. Again, he found them sleeping. Too weak to understand what was happening, too vulnerable to the wiles of God's enemy, they perhaps touched his pity, even there, even at that desperate juncture. He woke them a second time and warned them to pray against the world's temptations.

Returning to his Father, kneeling on that same stony ground once more, we knew his choice was made. Your will be done, not mine. The silent words were clear to us. It was the cry of his heart. But immediately the weight and pain of all the world's hatred and ugliness, violence and evil fell into his very soul. The gasp was real; the sweat broke from him. We yearned to release him. But we could no more save him from this destiny than we could save the fullness of our own fruits when they were squeezed in the olive press till good oil oozed not only from the soft flesh, but from the hard, nutty kernels at their core.

As Jesus grew increasingly aware of the way which lay ahead of him, as he felt more and more intensely the dread of lifting and carrying the terrible burden all the way through suffering and into death, his human frame began to shake. He bent forward, his hands on the rock supporting him, and drops of blood fell from his forehead to the ground. It seemed the very core of his heart would break at the prospect, at the depth and darkness of the deed he willed to perform. We feared for him, truly. A sigh rustled through us all in turn. It may have been the wind—perhaps a divine wind, a breath from heaven. For as the sigh faded, we perceived a new golden light beneath our boughs, and gradually, through the light, discerned a gold-winged angel, crouching at the side of Jesus.

The angel's huge wings folded, settled, half-embracing the figure of the Son of God. They stayed thus for long moments, and this time we could not hear if anything was being spoken. But we took comfort. There was a new sense of peace. In our dim way we joined ourselves with this strange and wonderful meeting. We prayed for strength for him. It took us longer to realise that the angel's calming influence had made a space and time for him to dwell on the knowledge that it was not simply loss he faced, not just a way of pain, anguish, shame and death, but a vast gift of love, from a deeper place than ever was plumbed before, and a pure recreation here on Earth, within humanity itself, of God's perfect love.

It was in silence that the angel left. Jesus lingered a while in more peaceful prayer, and then he rose unsteadily onto his feet, turned and crossed the garden once again, re-joining his disciples who, for a third time, had been overcome with weariness.

"Why are you still sleeping and taking your rest?" he questioned. "See— look over there—the hour is at hand. The Son of Man is betrayed into the hands of sinners."

The disciples had no sooner shaken themselves to wakefulness, than they saw, as we did, with shock and trepidation, a rapidly approaching band of men. A large and disorganised gang that drew ever closer, their swords and weapons catching the last faint gleams of daylight in the deepening gloom, their shouts sudden and ugly. Leading them, as we knew he had expected, was the half-crouching figure of Judas.

To the obvious dismay of his disciples, Jesus ignored their own panic and questions, turned away from them, and walked towards the approaching rabble.

Reflection

We stand in awe before Jesus' acceptance of his impending suffering. It is not something we feel we could ever contemplate imitating. But perhaps that is the point. None of us is capable of such profound and perfect obedience. It took the uniqueness of Christ to undertake to turn back the destructive years of Satan's influence; and even he needed the help of the angel. We are not called to imitate but to appreciate and venerate the saving love of our Lord. Yet we can, in our smaller way, follow his example. We can imitate Jesus' way of seeking a private place to spend time in prayer. We can strive to discover and to follow God's will, rather than our own ill-conceived plans or selfish desires. We can endeavour to accept pain and difficulty in our own lives, rather than seek to avoid such things whenever possible, because we prefer an easy life. We can, like the trees, learn to sympathise with others' pain. The power of this First Sorrowful Mystery is surely meant to help us.

Prayer

Dear Jesus, we thank you, from the bottom of our hearts, for your obedient decision to be the Lamb of God, who takes away the sins of the world. Help us, in our weakness, to follow your example both in seeking to know the will of God in our own human situations, and in accepting with courage whatever suffering may come our way. Lead us to unite our pain with yours, so it may be an echo of the love of God for all humanity. May we appreciate and use fully the precious gift of prayer. Thank you for the presence and assistance of our guardian angels. Amen

2. The Scourging at The Pillar

There is no avoiding the violence in this Mystery. It is a horrendously barbaric scene. Its impact on those who witnessed it must have been deep and lasting. It should be no less so on ourselves, because the pain and injury Jesus endured are the measure of what he was prepared to suffer out of love for us. He wanted us to know how much he loved us. Through his wounds we are saved. Although he could have saved himself, choosing to avoid this punishment, instead he opted to endure it. He gave his safety, his body, his blood, his life itself, so that we might be rescued from the clutches of sin and death.

Of all the witnesses who came to be with Jesus through his ordeal, surely Mary Magdalene must have been among those most affected by its cruelty.

Magdalene

A dense and raucous crowd was blocking any view of him by the time she arrived. She was hot and breathless from running so far to try to reach him. She owed him so much; she had to be there at this terrible hour, to support, to pray, just to be with him.

The watchers were craning forward, jeering, sometimes gasping—at the ferocity of the blows being inflicted, she presumed. She shuddered at their response. They were mostly men, but she was not going to let that stop her, having come so far. Mary Magdalene pushed and squeezed her way through them towards the front. It seemed to take a long time. Every time she made some progress, ruffians pushed her out of the way. She fell to the ground at one point, but scrambled to her feet again, flung back her tumbled hair and stared at them angrily. Eventually she broke through to the front and saw for herself what was happening.

Jesus had been stripped half-naked. His hands were bound with thick, ugly ropes around the pillar, and he was bloodied from head to foot. He could scarcely stand, but his head was still held defiantly high. Then the scourge, with its multiple strands and innumerable sharp black hooks, like the talons of vultures, came down across his back. The sound it made scored itself across her brain: the whistle of the thongs through the air; the sickening noise of their striking their target and tearing at the flesh of her dear Lord, Jesus. Mary's head reeled. She felt faint with horror.

For a while she could not bear to watch. She closed her eyes and prayed that God would send some kind of rescue. Surely this couldn't go on happening—not to Jesus, the holiest man who ever walked the Earth. God in heaven, help him! But even as she prayed, she heard the sounds, the terrible, repeated sounds of the scourges thrashing down onto his body again and again. Mary opened her eyes a crack and tried just to look at his hands. Tied mercilessly to the stone pillar, blood-spattered, those gentle hands were all she could bear to focus on. They were the hands that had touched her, long ago, in the beginning, when her life had changed. They were powerful hands, healing hands, loving hands. And now they were tethered, helpless against this brutal onslaught. The memories swirled in her mind as she struggled to focus simply on those hands. Her vision was strangely distorted, as if she gazed through flowing water.

Then Jesus staggered under the blows and an involuntary gasp began to escape his throat at each fresh impact. Hazily she saw him sink to his knees, his wrists dragged slowly downward against the stone pillar by the tightness of the ropes. And still the whips struck, over and over again.

It was too much to bear. She felt sick; she felt angry; she felt helpless. She cried out. "No—no! You can't do this! No!"

But the crowd hissed at her; someone pushed her again, almost to the ground. And a nearby guard turned towards her with an angry snarl. As she tried to get to her feet again, a stain of darkness clouded her sight and she fell a second time. Somehow, she seemed only half aware of her own struggle to lift herself up, a struggle which was clumsy and uncoordinated. She couldn't find her balance in the shadows which swayed within her consciousness. Then the darkness deepened, and utter blackness took its hold over her mind. She was not aware of falling, completely relaxed, onto the stony pavement.

As the scourging continued and the crowd pressed forward, she was kicked underfoot by some of the bystanders. But she felt nothing. Inside her mind Mary Magdalene was far away with Jesus on a bygone day.

Vividly she saw his face again: that face, just as she had first noticed it, when he caught sight of her in a crowd and turned back to look again. The expression in his eyes startled her afresh. He was the first man in years to look at her as though she was a human being of some value. He had glanced briefly at her, this stranger, and then turned back and looked again, gazing steadily into her eyes. There was genuine interest there, a spark of real concern. She was so used to calculation in men's eyes, to lust, scorn, derision, hatred. The care in the eyes of Jesus went through her like a bolt of lightning. Even so, she turned away. She couldn't believe that such care was real, or anything more than just a look. Or maybe it was trickery. She walked away from him.

Mary knew well she had a reputation. She was not respectable. No one ever spoke kindly to her. Yet here and now this stranger did. Undeterred by her turning away, he followed her, came up to her and spoke. He asked her questions about her life. At first, she resisted, not believing his motives could be as innocent as he seemed. But his questions showed he knew things about the course of her life already. She resisted a while longer. She accused him of spying on her. But at last, she became intrigued. There was something very different about this man. They walked to a quieter place and sat together and talked for a long time. Gradually she told him all her story. He never criticised. He emanated a kind of peace she had never known before.

"Who are you?" she asked at last.

"A man from Nazareth," he answered.

"You must be more than that," she protested. "How do you know so much? Why have you stayed talking with the likes of me for so long?"

"The likes of you?" he echoed.

"You know," she said, impatiently. "Embittered, dirty, downtrodden, ugly, worthless, lost."

"I'm here," he stated, "because you don't have to stay like that. I can save you from your sins and heal you of all that afflicts you."

"Really?" She spoke with some scorn.

"Would you like to be healed? Released from the bonds the evil one has fettered you with?"

She simply stared.

"I could cleanse you of your sin," he said, quite simply, as if this was normal conversation. "I could lift you out of shame and free you to know the real love of God."

"God?" she burst out. "God wants nothing to do with me. I'm a wretched specimen of humanity. Not worth the time of day."

"That's where you're wrong," he countered. "You are a child of God. And so am I. I will heal you and release you if you wish."

For a long time, she struggled with doubts and an instinctive mockery that rose up in her; yet his tone held something completely unfamiliar. She gazed into his face and sensed a kind of gentle power in him. What had she to lose?

"Do you wish to be released?" he asked patiently. She nodded, mute.

Mary saw it all again now within her mind. How he laid his gentle hands on her, murmuring words she did not try to understand. How she closed her eyes, almost swooning into a new daze of peacefulness. How, in a new authoritative voice, he commanded evil spirits to leave her, and she felt the knots of tension within her loosen one by one, allowing great burdens of darkness to slide from her body and from her mind. In those few moments—truly she had no idea how long it lasted—he cured her of everything that had gone so disastrously wrong in her life. Not only of disease but of the fear, and self-loathing and disgust and shame. And of the vile suspicious hostility that had taken possession of her which had been her only way to survive. But it had become like something living inside her, an antagonism to everything—compelling her, almost controlling her. His hands and his words drove it away. She knew real peace. A warmth of comfort filled her. She knew it was life changing.

At the end, when she opened her eyes to him, she felt lifted up, as if into fresh air. She still gazed into his face now, smiling at his new smile, breathing a different atmosphere. She still had that feeling, like a reborn child, as something thumped against her shoulder. She heard a noise of voices. What strange thing was this?

As Mary turned to see what was happening, she felt the texture of rough ground beneath her hands. She blinked at the stones and dirt before her eyes, seeing them only dimly and struggling to make sense of what she saw. She seemed to be lying spread-eagled on the ground. She raised her head and looked about, and daylight very gradually brought her mind back to the real world. People were moving away. Yes, it came back to her. She had been in a crowd. She had been watching some event. And then the terrible fact of where she was slammed into her brain. A weight of dread fell simultaneously into her stomach. She had been watching the fearful scourging of her beloved Saviour. She had seen his horrendous suffering and collapse under the savage execution of their punishment. Horror rose up within her. Where was he now?

She tried to rise to her feet. Her movement was awkward. She felt the bruising on her hands, in her back and on her legs and knees. She tried to shake back the hair which had fallen over her eyes but had to wipe it back with the fingers of one hand from where it had glued itself to her face. She felt the grains of dirt that clung to her skin. But at last, she was able to stand and look to the centre of the square. Jesus was on the ground, shoulders turned to one side. His face was towards her, but he was almost unrecognisable. One of the guards came up and doused him with a bucket of water to bring him back to full consciousness. Mary's hand rose to her mouth, as if to help contain the shock and sickness which rose in her like bile. They dragged him to his feet. Her beloved rescuer, friend and teacher—he was alone in their clutches; he was defenceless, defeated by their sheer physical brutality. How could it have happened? A helpless mixture of despair and rage flooded her. Tears stood in her eyes.

"Mary, what happened to you?"

"Were you on your own?"

Some of the other women who followed Jesus had spotted Mary Magdalene from across the square, and now that the crowd had thinned, had managed to come across to help the friend who, they could see, was even more visibly shaken than themselves.

"Whatever happened to you?" they repeated.

Mary made no answer for a while. What had happened to her was as nothing next to the agony that had been meted out to Jesus.

"I must have fainted," she said.

"You poor soul." It was Joanna who took her arm. "Come on. Let us take care of you. There's nothing more we can do here."

She wanted to stay, but she knew it was useless. So as the hefty soldiers, one on each side, dragged Jesus away in one direction, she let the women lead her away in the other. But her mind was scarcely paying them any attention. She was still trying to understand how it could have happened. To Jesus—the most amazing, good, gifted, holy person in the world. He had brought her a new life. He had rescued her from a kind of living torment. She had come to believe he really was the Messiah people spoke about, that he was even the Son of God himself. She thought he was destined to lead everyone into new life. And now he had been brought down, like a hunted animal. He was powerless to save himself. It made no sense. And it meant that all their hopes were crashing down.

As her friends helped her to bathe and dress in fresh clothes, Mary's feeling gradually settled into a profound despair. Tears welled in her eyes, and then ran helplessly down her cheeks. All was lost. The light of her new life was abruptly extinguished. It seemed to her the whole world had gone dark.

Reflection

Our Lord here suffered pain beyond imagining. He did it for us. Mary of Magdala saw it only as a desperately unjust end of all their hopes, but later she, like us, from our totally altered age, learnt of the saving value of Christ's Passion. Let us never cease to appreciate the depth of his love which could embrace such suffering. We so often allow our minds to grow dull and memories to fade. This is perhaps why, in her wisdom, the Church takes us through Lent and Easter every year, to remember the goodness of God in facing such terrors out of love for us. We should never cease to stand with the witnesses of the very day it happened. Like them we should stand with our Lord. And we should be ready to bear our own trials when they come, in whatever shape or form, because it is a way we share his experience. A way of loving him. A way of giving ourselves as a minor contribution to his constant ongoing spiritual battle to save the world from sin and death, and to save souls from hell.

Prayer

Father in heaven, do not let our hearts grow callous and forgetful of your only Son's suffering for our salvation. Help us to be constant in standing with Jesus, and with all who suffer any kind of loss or pain, especially those persecuted for their Christian faith in this modern world. Help us to accept our own trials and to join them with those of your precious Son. Bless us all, dear God, with an increasing understanding of the depth and infinite giving which is your love. We praise you and thank you, dearest Jesus, for your obedience to the Father, and for the saving power of your cruel wounds. Amen

3. The Crowning with Thorns

This third Sorrowful Mystery leaves behind the emphasis on the physical brutality of Jesus' treatment for a while to turn to a more psychological kind of abuse—the taunting and gloating of his captors over their victim now that they have him in a weakened state. It is the lashes of mockery that assault him now: mockery of his Kingship, with the crowning of his head with a circlet of fierce thorns. Jesus accepts it all, quietly asserting only that "My Kingdom is not of this world". A meaningless phrase to them, perhaps, but a profound truth for us. Then he is dragged into public view and his freedom put at the mercy of the crowd. A crowd? Or an angry mob? What must it have been like to stand amongst them?

A Mother's Son

For years I'd stood by my wild, curly-headed boy, watching with occasional spells of anxiety as his childhood pranks developed into more serious offences. "He'll grow up," I used to say. "He'll see the error of his ways. When he meets a good woman and settles down."

I couldn't have been more wrong. The women he got involved with were not the kind to settle him down. Even when some rival group of ne'er-do-wells beat him up, it didn't halt his downward spiral. He went from petty crimes to serious violence. The first time he went to jail I nearly broke my heart. You still love them, you see. You still think: one day he'll change into the decent boy you always hoped he'd be.

There were some better days. When he got out the first time he came home for a few weeks. It built my hopes up. I prayed and prayed. But it was only to have those fragile hopes dashed again. So, when he was jailed with his rebels that year, I wiped him out of my mind. He had done truly terrible things. I couldn't bear the thought of them. So, I decided not to think of my son at all. For weeks I forgot all about him.

And then one of my neighbours came knocking excitedly at the door, mid-afternoon. When I opened it, wiping the flour from my arms, old Benjamin stood there, his big, knuckled hand waving in the direction of the square.

"It's release time!" he shouted.

I must have looked blank because he came a step closer, thrust his bearded chin into my face and shouted again.

"Release time! When they free one of the prisoners for the festival! They're calling for your Barabbas to be let out!"

"No," I said, a dread taking hold of me. "Never. There must be plenty more deserving. He's a rogue, my Barabbas. A villain."

"There is someone else," Benjamin admitted. "But rogues pull the crowds, you know. I think he might get out."

"I don't want him to get out," I cried. The old man was slow to comprehend. "I don't want all the problems to start all over again. Who's the 'someone else'?"

"This Jesus from Nazareth."

"Jesus? The prophet who healed the lame beggar? The one who brought the evil spirits out of Martha's boy down the road?"

"The same," answered Benjamin, more slowly. "He was even supposed to have brought a dead girl back to life. So they say," he added. "But the officials don't like it. Too much of a threat to their authority."

"But he's not a criminal!"

"He's been arrested, all the same. Handed over to the masters from Rome. Punished by a flogging. Pontius Pilate's been out on the balcony asking the crowd if they want him to be freed."

I stared at him. I had heard so much about this Jesus. Martha had told me how he saved her boy. He didn't have the fits now. No more throwing himself about the room, scaring them to death. She'd been like a different woman since that day. I even saw him myself once, a couple of years back, when I was walking through the Temple colonnade. There he was, sitting talking to a crowd that had gathered round him. I couldn't stop myself from lingering. Such a voice. And simple words. Simple words, you know, but deep. He didn't see me, but he set me thinking all right. Jesus – been arrested?

"He's the one they should set free, isn't he?" I declared. Benjamin laughed. "Why are you laughing?"

"Come and see for yourself. I think it's your rogue they'll choose."

"Just wait a minute," I said, turning to untie my apron and grab my shawl from the peg on the wall. If Benjamin was right, someone had to stand against such injustice. These men! They needed their heads knocking together.

Ten minutes later we came out of the alleyway onto the road that dropped down into the square. I caught a glimpse of the robed figure of the governor moving across the balcony. Between him and us was a jostling and raucous crowd. The noise was huge. My heart seemed to stop.

"Crucify him! Crucify him!" they shouted over and over, in rolling waves of sound. "Crucify him! Set Barabbas free!"

My blood ran cold, and my hand came up to my mouth. There were women as well as men, young and old, in these surging masses in the square. Fists shook in the air. I suddenly felt afraid. What was I doing here, the mother of this man they wanted to set free, unless it was to join their clamour for his release? And that was something I could never do. What was there in Barabbas that so attracted them? His reckless spirit? His evil and violence? I thought of his hands—red with the blood of the victims murdered by his troop of rebels. They were so wrong, so wrong!

"Come on," urged Benjamin, plunging into the crowd to get nearer to the front.

But I let the old man disappear into the throng. I had no desire to draw attention to myself. What would they do if I raised my voice against his release? If I spoke out for Jesus? My throat went dry at the thought. My heart had tightened into a painful knot. There could be no arguing against the passion of this frenzied mob.

The figure of Pilate the governor was moving back again across the balcony of the Praetorium, and another figure slowly followed. I thought at first it was one of the governor's underlings. Then Pilate looked up and his voice echoed round the walls of the square:

"Do you want me to release the king of the Jews?"

It was Jesus there beside him. I could tell, just from the cautious way he moved, in pain from the flogging, and then the way he stood, limp-shouldered, slightly bent, yet gazing steadily forward, unprotesting. They had dressed him in a purple robe and put something on his head. Twisted thorns, it might have been; it was hard to tell from a distance. But lines of blood ran from the puncture wounds it must have made in his poor, innocent head. It was Jesus— and they were baying for his blood.

"Shall I release him to you?"

Angry shouts rose from the crowd. "No! Crucify him! We want Barabbas!"

I shrank into the shadows. Fine woman I was. Coming here all puffed up with righteousness, thinking I had the strength to stand up for justice. I cowered there, like a feeble girl. I hadn't even the courage to slip away, in case anyone noticed and realised who I was. I drew my shawl up over my head, and there I stayed, paralysed by disgust with myself.

I made no move when my Barabbas was brought out. I saw him distantly, in the gaps between people's heads, as they released him from his chains. His fellow collaborators gathered around him, whooping in celebration, eventually carrying him off shoulder high. Some people followed them; but others stayed, still determined on the prophet's execution. Pilate was going to hand him over to the soldiers for a brutal, slow and shameful death by crucifixion. I was held there by the horror of this impending suffering. How could they free a man who had murdered innocents, and scourge and kill a holy man who had only healed the sick and spoken the greatest truths we ever heard?

I had to stay. In fact, as the crowd thinned a little, I drifted slowly forward with those remaining. It was less dangerous now and I wanted to be closer to the place where he had stood. As I hovered there, close under the balcony, I was struck by the thought that, like my Barabbas, this Jesus was some mother's son—though so unlike Barabbas in every other way. What must that woman be feeling? Perhaps she was here, held, paralysed like me, powerless. A wave of sudden sympathy for her unknotted my heart. I found myself praying for her. I deserved disgrace, but she…? She deserved my heartfelt prayers, and I was so preoccupied by her plight, that I was only vaguely aware that a crowd was gathering around the pillared entrance doorway not far from where I stood.

Everything happened at once. Shouts broke out again as soldiers came out through the doorway, thrusting Jesus forward in the midst of them, down the steps. Just as it was dawning in my mind that they were already taking him off to his final execution, I saw her face. Opposite me, across the space they had cleared for the soldiers to pass through, supported by a little group, was the figure of his mother. It was obvious from her dignity, from the harrowed features, from the love and desperation written in her face. As if to confirm it, Jesus turned so he could gaze at her. He must have seen the shining tears in her eyes. The soldiers pushed him on.

It brought tears to my eyes, too, just at the moment that it happened. Jesus had turned his head slightly towards our side of the crowd, and he had almost passed by when his eyes swivelled fully round to meet mine. He looked at me. I can't describe the flow of heat that travelled through me, nor the expression in his eyes. The face was troubled, ashen, but his eyes flared with incredible love. There was none of the scorn in them that I deserved. He knew. It left me breathless. He knew precisely who I was. He understood the confusion of grief and shame in having a son like Barabbas, and there was forgiveness, not condemnation, in his heart. All my torment dropped away, as though he had lifted me above everything.

Even in a terrible moment like that, going to his death, when he knew my son had been released in his stead, he wanted me to know he cared. He had love, even for me.

A man, a prophet, or even more? I had always been a little dubious when people claimed he was divine. But he had looked into my eyes, and I had looked into his, and I knew. As Martha had so full-heartedly declared, this Jesus was the Son of God.

Reflection

This mother has witnessed neither the scourging nor the crowning with thorns of our Lord, and perhaps is the least likely person to show him any sympathy, much less to understand anything of his other-worldly Kingdom. Yet she, like many others, has found herself attracted by him, and by the stories of his healings and miracles. So, although she does not dare vocally to oppose the mob, she is driven by a desire to draw closer to him, and ultimately experiences a deep though wordless moment of communication with him which confirms her instinctive response. She, the mother of the criminal Barabbas, is touched by the gaze of Jesus into a sense of his mystery, his difference from everyone, his divinity. For a while she stands on the threshold of the Kingdom of God, and she realises that what his gaze confers is love.

Prayer

We praise you, Jesus, for the humble obedience with which you submitted to the jibes and mockery of those incapable of understanding the nature of your Kingdom. Lamb of God, you submitted without protest, knowing you were fulfilling the will of your Father in heaven. You never ceased to love even your persecutors, even the mother of Barabbas. We pray that we may learn to imitate such patient obedience, and that we may, with the help of your grace, reject the instinct to retaliate against those who cause us offence. Teach us to trust you always and not to mind what others think of us. We pray also for all those in our world today who suffer persecution because of their faith in you. Thank you for their amazing witness, dear Lord. Finally, we pray for those people today who mock your Church because they have never come to understand your nature and your saving love. Have mercy on them, Jesus. Amen

4. The Carrying of The Cross

It goes beyond the power of words to describe the barbarity of this act of forcing an injured and weakened Jesus to carry the burden of the instrument of his own coming death all the way along the route to Golgotha. God, mercifully, provided some assistance in the shape of Simon of Cyrene, who helped to carry the cross part of the way, and some sympathy from women, particularly his mother who watched and walked with him, but also from Veronica and other women of Jerusalem. But the cruelty of his suffering persisted, remorseless and unrelieved right to the end. The jeering bystanders and the Roman perpetrators of this punishment, one might feel, must have had no hearts at all. One of them, in this story, recalls what it was like for him to be there.

Old Soldier

She helps me ease my aged bones down into the bench. Then stands, hands on hips, gazing at me with an air of satisfaction.

"Thank you," I say. "You can leave me now, Livia."

She turns with a little grunt away from me and moves off towards her household duties, and maybe a trip to the market. I'm more than happy to stay where she has put me. Blissful sunshine warms this corner of the neglected orchard. I look up through tattered autumn trees, gnarled and gaunt now, just like me. Yet the sun glints on one or two lingering apples; and beyond I can see the softer shapes and the peaceful green of my neighbour's olive orchard on the rising slope of the hillside.

It was my father's smallholding, this place, before it was mine. A lively farm in days of yore. Not grand of course. We were of humble stock really, settled in our small villa some few miles away from Assisi in Italy. It prospered in our day too. My wife, Carinia, loved the outdoor life, the constant bustle and vigour of the work, the healthy glow in our children's faces, fed straight from the land and from the work of our hands.

All that has faded into the past, though, now. We took on a servant, Livia, a widow from the village, to help Carinia when she fell sick. Now there's only me and Livia left here. She cares for me well enough, and day follows day in a well-worn and comfortable routine. But I grow feebler as the days grow shorter and the heat in the sun weakens. I think perhaps I am not long for this world.

Livia has left a rug beside me, in case I should feel chilled. But I can feel the warmth of the sunlight on my limbs, and I gaze thankfully at the glow lighting the soft, old skin and sparse hairs of my forearm. Slowly it takes me back. My thoughts drift in a familiar direction. I think of someone else's arm I touched once, years ago. Old memories. I let myself wander through them yet again. I lapse into that past time.

I was a different fellow then: a soldier, big, bluff, frightened of nothing, serving my time in the Roman army, despatched overseas. I was in a cohort serving in Judaea at the time, under Herod, but seconded to the governor in Jerusalem. I wasn't even supposed to be on duty on that day and had been intending to write a letter home to Carinia. But Marcus, a fellow soldier, went down with a fever and I stood in for him.

"What are we doing?" I asked one of the soldiers, as we hurried on our way, responding to a summons to the Praetorium.

"The usual, I suppose," came his reply. "Taking villains to Golgotha. Crucifixions, I expect."

This was not my usual territory, but I said nothing. I could do it as well as any man, I supposed. Death was nothing new to soldiers, after all. And although crucifixion was a ghastly way to die, they were villains when all was said and done. It was probably only giving them back what they had done to others.

So, I marched with the detail up the rising track at the rear of the straggling procession towards Golgotha without a qualm. All in a day's work, I thought. Soon it would be over, and I'd get back to writing to my dear Carinia. Even when we had to halt because the last of the three prisoners had fallen under his cross, I spared no thought for him.

I was glad not to be given the actual job of nailing the criminals to their crosses, as other soldiers were summoned forth to take the nails and the hammers and pinion the first two healthy-looking rogues to the wooden beams of the crosses which were then set to left and right of the site known as the place of the skull. One of the criminals screamed as the cross was set in its place, while the other's face wore a set grimace. People were jeering behind us. I hoped they would make haste with the third one and get it all over, and my eyes were looking over towards him when my name was harshly called together with those of other companions beside me. We were trained to obey, and I stepped forward promptly, even though something grim took a hold on my heart like a clenched fist.

This fellow was different. I noticed it as soon as I got a good look at him. He seemed already broken, exhausted. The scars lacing his skin bore testimony to a heavy flogging. He had thorn branches twisted round his head in a mockery of a crown and there was dried blood on his face from the wounds they had made. He drew particularly loud, scornful jeers and curses from the crowd. Some of them shouted mockingly, "King of the Jews!!"

But he was meekly compliant. He lay down for us without protest. There was neither anger nor fear in his eyes. One of my fellow soldiers held his arm in place and they passed the hammer to me.

I did it swiftly, telling myself it was my duty. I had no choice. I remember closing my eyes as I grasped the fellow's wrist and drove the nail home. I remember vowing that I would never write to Carinia about this. I remember his voice speaking, though I could not take in the words he said. But it made me open my eyes and look at him. Immediately it seemed his eyes held mine. Yes, there was pain in them, but something deeper too. A darkness and a warmth. It seemed to wash right into me, like a warm tide shifting the cold boulder of pain which had grown in my heart. I swallowed hard and turned my head away.

Ridiculous, I thought. This was just a job, and it was done. Others had nailed his left hand and his feet in place and now the cross was being lifted into its position on the summit of the mound of Golgotha. I walked away, vowing to forget. I will never think of this again, I said to myself, as we formed into ranks and prepared to march back to the Praetorium.

I kept my promise never to speak of this to Carinia. But as to forgetting—it proved impossible. It haunted me. And one of my fellow soldiers, who had heard the words our victim spoke, told me about them.

"He asked his Father to forgive you."

"He… what?" I gaped, disbelieving.

"It was his God he was addressing, I presume. He said, 'Father forgive them for they know not what they do.'"

Since then, those healing words and that remembered dark gaze of his eyes have never left me. I faked nonchalance to the rest of the cohort, of course. I served out my time as a trusty, unquestioning Roman soldier. But inside me the impression he had left refused to fade.

I am lost in it now as I sit peacefully among these old familiar trees. I wonder again over the strangeness of it all. I wonder just who he was? All the rumours of the time had made no sense to me. And yet he came so close. Almost as if he knew me more intimately than the people who lived around me, those I'd known all down the years. How could that be? I have no answers. Yet I'm glad to ponder over and over again on all the questions.

The breeze is light today, and the shadows creep only slowly up and down the twisted trees as their patchwork crosses the orchard landscape. I lapse, as I often do, into a semi-doze in the cooling sun. I gaze into his face. Time slows. It must be hours since Livia left me here. But no matter. I am with him. I want nothing more.

Reflection

We might imagine the Roman soldiers to be unthinking brutes, but in this story the soldier proves to be a man of some sensitivity in his ordinary life. The strict discipline of the Roman army, however, binds him into obedience of orders, even if they lead to involvement in the nailing of a victim to the cross on which he is doomed to die. What stays with him ever afterwards is his memory of Jesus, the pathos of his wounded figure, the depth of his gaze and the meaning of the words he spoke. This victim's forgiveness for his captors and executioners gives this old soldier an unending fascination with Jesus, and an unreasoning hope of one day being close to him again. He is changed, like the mother of Barabbas, by an experience, however brief, of the Lord's forgiveness and love.

Prayer

Dearest Lord Jesus, who struggled to carry your heavy and painful cross in order to save all of us, your forgiveness for your persecutors is beyond our understanding. Forgive us for all the times when we have not borne our trials with patience, and those when we have not forgiven those who have hurt us. Deepen in us, Jesus, the understanding that your huge work of carrying on the cross all humanity's sins, is an undertaking that we must continue in our own time and in our own way through opportunities which you give us. Let us learn to offer our own pains and crosses in penance for the darkness in humanity and for all our sins. Amen

5. The Crucifixion

All the fierce cruelty and derision inflicted on Jesus culminate here. These are the last hours and minutes of his life. This is the ending of God's dwelling in human flesh and sharing in our world. The hanging of the wounded Jesus on a criminal's cross, with nails through his hands and feet, is horrific, though apparently an entertainment for the mocking multitude. It brings total despair for those of his followers who had hoped for a conquest of the Roman regime and a Messiah who would reign in glory. It is hard to watch. Indeed, most of his followers flee. Yet those who knew him most closely and loved him most intensely choose to stay close throughout his agonising ordeal.

Beneath the Cross

My fellow disciples were sick with disappointment and terrified of the future. How could this have happened? What sense was there in this? They were desperate.

"Come away, John. Come with us!"

"We can do no good here."

"We are in danger if we stay, surely."

"Come away, John, before it's too late!"

Their voices made a clamour in my head. They even grabbed at my arm, at my clothes, trying to drag me with them. I could understand their way of thinking. I would not stop them. Let them go. But I could not leave this place. I stayed with him. I stood near him through all those long hours that he hung on the cross of shame in Golgotha. I could be nowhere else. My life was here. He was here—my Lord, my Christ, my everything. I loved him; and he me.

I watched him die. Oh, there was ugliness—in those great nails they had driven through his hands and feet; in the angry, jeering shouts of the crowd. But he—he had a beauty, despite all they had done to him. A strange beauty of passivity. Even the wounds on his body, inflicted with such hatred, he accepted, absorbed; they had become a part of him. They had a kind of beauty which I could not name. Because he bore them unresistingly, perhaps. The Lamb of God. Even now, in this fearful place, I adored and worshipped him.

He was mute through most of those crawling hours. I know he must have prayed and suffered and endured. I could not begin to imagine his pain. When he spoke to the more sympathetic thief at his side, on one of the crosses which stood to either side of his own, I could see the effort it took, the huge cost. He closed his eyes afterwards and his breath came hard. I prayed for God to ease his agony, to grant him peace. Perhaps it was not even a prayer, just an ache in the heart. There were no words for this.

There were not many of us who stayed with him there. Even some who came were so afraid of the authorities they lurked at a good distance. As the shadows gathered and the hours passed, they were scarcely visible. But I could see the group of women right in front of his cross. The wife of Clopas was there, and Mary Magdalene, on her knees. And at the heart of the group was Mary, the mother of our Lord. She stood upright, despite the exhaustion she must have felt, and her eyes gazed steadily on her son. Her face was lined now with coming age, and shadowy in the increasing darkness. But there was a glitter in her eyes: a gleam of reflected light, from some source invisible to the rest of us. Perhaps a glint of tears, or an edge of unwilling bitterness. She had seen so much. Who could know what she was feeling? Yet her head was held high, looking up to her son, being with him in every second, sharing everything, her gaze unfaltering. Her heart must have been anguished. Her whole life had been his life, I thought. She would be lost after this.

As I looked back to the figure on the cross, to the face of Jesus, I saw that his eyes were open again, and their expression was of care and sadness mingled. They came to rest on the face of his mother. I think she must have felt the love he gave her in that long look. There was just a tightening of the lips on her part, a faint smile. But she did not stir.

"Woman," his voice was low, but perfectly audible. It transfixed me. I held my breath. "This is your son."

He turned his gaze to me. My heart swelled in me, touched by the silent love so eloquent in those dark eyes. So familiar now. His dear and precious eyes; so soon to be closed by death for ever.

"My beloved disciple," he spoke again. My throat was constricted now; I could not speak. Tears misted my sight of him. "This is your mother."

I gave a silent nod of consent. Maybe he saw the tears fall from me. I heard again his heavy drawing of breath. I glanced across at Mary. She had turned to me. Tears stood in her eyes too.

I took the few strides needed to reach her, lurching a little on the rocky ground. I laid a hand on her shoulder. She did not move, so I drew close beside her, offering my hand. She took it in hers—a chill grasp—and we stayed like that, hand in hand, leaning together, as the last hour slowly turned. The world grew dark as night.

When his voice came again, it was little more than a croak. "I thirst."

They offered him the vinegar-soaked sponge, held aloft on a hyssop stick, and perhaps he drank. There was no sound. No sound at all.

"It is accomplished," Jesus uttered, his voice hoarse and weak, the words his last. He died at that ninth hour before our eyes, giving up his spirit in a last faint exhalation. It was scarcely perceptible. Just a slight fall of the shoulders, a small sinking, and a deeper drooping of his head. He was gone.

For a while there was a profound silence. My heart seemed caught in a tight grasp, in a kind of fierce spasm. For a second, I thought perhaps my life would end at the same moment. But although the hard pain in my heart endured, nothing else changed. My vision remained clear; my strength endured. Some of the soldiers were just beginning to stir, and people to murmur, when a huge bolt of lightning split the black sky in two. All the faces, gathered round that ghastly place, were brightly lit for a fleeting moment and shadows fell across the ground from the three crosses. Then the scene plunged once again into darkness. We felt the ground shake beneath our feet. It brought shouts of panic from the people; some began to run away. A centurion stood boldly and declared that this was indeed the Son of God. Mary heard. She reached forward as if to speak to him, but he melted swiftly into the shadow. Others stood awed and spoke in breathless whispers. I felt Mary trembling and put my arm around her. She was frail and cold. I took off my cloak and draped it round her.

"Thank you, John," she said gently, amazingly composed.

My arm, around her shoulders, gave her the lightest squeeze. "I will be a son to you now," I said.

She turned to look at me. "And I a mother to you."

She reached up with one hand to my face, and that hard tension in my heart was suddenly released. I leant against her, and we held one another in a clumsy half-embrace for a while, my head on her shoulder, her arm around me.

What a gift he gave to each of us, just at that blackest of hours. So, our grief was softened by this sudden change in our relationship. Or perhaps it was deepened, because we were free to share it, as we leant into one another's warmth, admitting this unthinkable loss, allowing tears to flow, while others roused themselves and talked and moved and gathered into new groups, discussing what had happened, and many shifted off towards the town. We lingered before the now-lifeless form, the mute beauty of the body she had given him, and in which God had lived on Earth. We did not want to take our eyes from the pale, sculpted grace of his figure, his closed eyes, the peace written in his features. There was loveliness still, in every part of him.

We stayed a long time together, until the guards came to check the bodies, making sure they could be removed in plenty of time for the Sabbath. Not many remained to see the breaking of the legs of the two unfortunate victims on the crosses either side of our Lord. I think we both looked away, although the sounds of blows and shouts rang in our ears. They had no need to deal with our Lord, Jesus, since he had died many minutes earlier. Yet, as I watched, anxious that they should not molest the sleeping and holy remains of Christ, one of the soldiers pierced his side with a lance. Instantly, blood and water poured from the wound. My gasp made Mary look up too.

Both of us watched this outpouring. It shocked us, held us, astonished us by its flooding abundance. My anger melted into awe—and that, more slowly, into love. It was as though he still lived, still gave of himself, out of very death.

I don't know what Mary's thoughts were as we stayed on the same spot, rooted, spellbound. I had had that brief moment of fear, earlier, that this was to be the end of everything—my own death too. But now I knew that this was not to be an ending after all. He had given us each other, and he had given us a future. He had given us treasure to value and to ponder on. He had given us the outpouring wealth of love. Perhaps it was forgiveness, too, forgiveness of all who had hounded and captured him and brought him down. I knew we needed to pray. And I suspect Mary's thoughts were not dissimilar. So, we clung on there in the intense cold, drawing warmth from one another, until all the crowds had melted away.

We saw Joseph of Arimathea and Nicodemus, coming up the hill with funeral cloths and jars of spices and ointments. I praised God silently for their faith and their loyalty. We watched until at last they brought the body of Jesus Christ down from his bloodied cross and prepared him for burial in an unused tomb.

Reflection

For all the horror in this story, something else surmounts it. It is not, for all, the total defeat which everyone expected and over which many of his followers despaired. It is desperately sad for those who love him deeply. Yet Mary, his mother, knows a love for her Son which keeps her steadfast here, as it has done through the thirty years of his life. John, the beloved disciple, despite his grief, is touched by both an unexpected beauty, and the first inklings of perception that this ending would also bring a new beginning.

They must have felt numb. They cannot, surely, have understood at this time the enormity of the changes that the future was to bring. Yet, as they silently accept the loving direction of Jesus to be mother and son for one another, they inaugurate a new order: the beginning of the burgeoning role of Mary's motherhood and the belonging of John and all disciples to her as the heart of a new family. Maybe we could say that this moment plants a seed of the future church. It is certainly a moment in which love remains undefeated. Jesus, even in death, pours out his loving grace in the tangible form of his blood, mingled with water. His Mother and his beloved disciple share a love which is infinitely deepened by the sorrow and pain they experience.

Prayer

Beloved Lord, it was for our sakes that you poured out your loving mercy, your blood, your very life on the cross. Help us in our small ways to give of ourselves in love and mercy to others. Expand our hearts and our capacity to love and to forgive. May we obtain the strength and wisdom we need to make our sorrows one with yours, and help us carry your cross to the end, offering everything to you and praying for all those who suffer injustice and violence in our day. We pray especially, Lord, for those followers of yours who in this current time suffer relentless persecution, cruelty and sometimes death for their faith. Praise you, Lord, today and always. Amen

The Glorious Mysteries

1. The Resurrection

This first Glorious Mystery opens in the darkness of loss and despair. The future hopes of the Lord's followers seem to be destroyed. There is no way they can imagine continuing their journey of discipleship without the inspiration, the leadership and the presence of their teacher and shepherd, Jesus Christ. The thoughts of Mary Magdalene and the other women turn away from the empty future and look backwards to him, and thus to caring for the body he has left behind. They have dutifully waited over the long hours of the Sabbath day, and now they are fully prepared with all the spices needed to honour the body·of the Lord. They have no idea what awaits them!

Discovery

I could not visit his tomb on the Sabbath, of course. I ached to be there. It was unbearable that he was gone—this wonderful, holy man who had so completely changed my life. But it was almost as unbearable that his body lay alone in that dark tomb in such a lonely place. I wanted to be there to grieve fully for him. It was what he deserved and all I wanted to do. The rest of life was suddenly worthless. That Sabbath was the longest I ever lived through.

How the next days, weeks and months were to be borne was something I dared not even begin to think about.

Mary, young James' mother, guessed what was in my heart and mind. She offered to accompany me to the tomb of Jesus early the next morning. So we were up before dawn the next day and reached the site just as dawn was breaking. It was shadowy everywhere, but a pinkish light picked out the tops of the hills. There was dew on the ground still, and the sweet smell of the night time lingered. Mary and I were carrying the spices with which we planned to anoint the body of our Lord. We were not at all sure if we would be able, between us, to shift the stone which blocked the grave's entrance. But if it proved impossible, we would go back and fetch some of the disciples to help us.

It was still so dark that it was not until we drew really close to the tomb, that we saw something strange. The stone lay on its side. The mouth of the cave yawned open. Both of us hesitated. Was this some kind of trap? Had the authorities taken him, before we could bestow any care upon him? Instinctively we clasped hands and whispered.

"How could this have happened?"

"Might someone be inside, waiting to catch us?"

"Why should they?"

"Let's go quietly and peep inside."

So, we laid down the jars as noiselessly as we could and tiptoed towards the open tomb. There was no one on watch just inside the entrance, so we went closer. We still saw no one. We reached the very entrance at last without finding anyone on guard.

"Let's look inside," Mary said to me, "and then we'll fetch the ointment and spices for him."

So, we stepped boldly into the darkness of the tomb. It was chill and lightless and for a while we could see nothing. As our eyes adjusted to the dark, we expected to see clearly where the body of our dear Jesus lay. But again, it was strange. More than strange. We saw the white cloths, the burial cloths, but of our Lord there was no sign. The stone where he should have lain was bare. The shock grew slowly in my heart until settling like a cold, lumpy knot within me. I had waited so long for this moment, and now the tomb which should have kept him safe was empty. We searched every corner, but apart from the burial clothes there was no sign of the precious, wounded, crucified body of our Lord.

"He's been taken," I said, shocked and disbelieving. "How could that be?"

"Who would do such a thing?"

"Pilate's soldiers, I suppose. Perhaps. But why? And where would they have they put him?"

For a while longer we stayed there, pointlessly. I think it was just that we couldn't believe what our eyes were seeing. We both touched the stone where he had been placed; Mary first, as if to make sure her eyes were not deceiving her, and then I knelt beside it and placed both hands on it, because it was the nearest thing that we could touch now to Jesus himself. I prayed in silence for him—but it was hard. My heart was desolate.

"Perhaps we could still anoint him," Mary said then. "If we could find out where he is. Do you think the soldiers would let us?"

"Well, we need to find out where they've taken him, first, don't we?" I remembered the brothers all at once. They would want to know about this. "Come on," I urged, "we'd better tell the others what's happened."

Abandoning our jars and spices, we ran back to find the disciples and alert them to this alarming turn of events. They were amazed, of course. Maybe they doubted our tale. I couldn't blame them. I wouldn't have believed it if I hadn't seen for myself.

"Leave it to us," John said, and grabbing Peter to go with him, he set off at a run.

Mary and I waited a while and then went to tell the story to the other women. Mary joined them in their simple breakfast preparations, but I wanted to go back and stay near his burial place while Peter and John searched. It was the nearest I could get to him, after all. I felt a huge need just to be with him again. He had saved me, loved me, taught me so much. I had poured ointment over his feet once before in deep gratitude, and he had commented that I had prepared him for his burial. Now it was all I could think about—the need to do everything I could to honour him. He was the meaning of my life now. Nothing but the loss of him mattered to me. I wanted a place to grieve.

The morning was lighter as I retraced my steps. There was birdsong, but I didn't listen. It seemed inappropriate, somehow. I would have liked a total silence. When I arrived, everything was just the same. The big stone lay turned onto its side, and the entrance to the tomb gaped wide. I stood nearby. It was the best I could do—the closest thing I could find to being with him. I would never see him again. Perhaps I would never even see his body again. Tears came easily and I let them run down my face. I grieved for everything – not just for the loss of him, but for all his agonising journey, from his trial to the scourging at the pillar, from the public humiliation at the Praetorium to the carrying of his cross to Calvary. And for the pain and anguish of his crucifixion. Too terrible. Too cruel. I wept.

When my sobbing eased a little, I wiped my face on the long veil I was wearing and decided I would venture into the tomb again. I just wanted to kneel one more time by the stone where he had lain, to touch the last place that he had touched. My love for him would never die.

I stepped into the tomb, expecting only darkness within, but there was a sudden burst of light. Panic ran through me like fire. I shielded my eyes against the brightness. What was this? As my eyes cleared, I could see two large creatures, men—or were they angels? —seated in loose, long, white clothing at each end of the stone. They had clear, fine faces and they glowed golden with some interior light. Once over the surprise I felt no fear of them. Their garments fluttered in a breeze—there was movement about them. It took me several moments of gazing to realise that they must indeed be angels, and their movement, the light breeze came from their shifting wings. Then one of them spoke.

"Woman," he said—a beautiful voice too, "Why are you weeping?"

I wiped my face again and stepped a little closer. I felt I could trust them with my life.

"They have taken my Lord away," I explained, "and I don't know where they have put him."

The one who had not spoken glanced suddenly towards the tomb entrance, and I think there was a slight noise at the same time, like a step outside in the garden. So, I turned too, wondering if perhaps the disciples had returned. I could see the garden outside, its colours lit by the early sunshine. I caught sight fleetingly of a man passing by. Not one of the disciples, and not coming towards the grave. Perhaps he was a gardener. I turned back to the angels, wondering if I could rush out to catch the man. Maybe he had seen what happened here? The angels nodded their agreement with gentle smiles. I slipped away, out of the mouth of the cave into the daylight. I saw the man again and made my way towards him.

As I drew near, I could see that he was quite tall, wearing a long grey robe, with a hood over his head. It cast his face into shadow, so I could not make out if his expression was friendly. I would take a chance though. It was my only hope. I was about to speak, when he accosted me first.

"Woman," he said, strangely echoing the angel, "why are you weeping? Who is it you are looking for?"

I gestured at the mouth of the grave. "Oh sir," I said," if you have taken him away, please tell me where you have put him, and I will go and remove him."

Instead of answering straightaway, he came a little closer, and I saw his eyes seeking mine. "Mary!" he said.

I knew the voice; I knew the eyes then. But my mind reeled. It couldn't be!

"Rabbuni!" I gasped.

He lowered the hood then, and I saw clearly that it was Jesus himself. Tears broke from me again, but not of sorrow this time. Tears of amazed joy. But how…?

"I don't understand," I said.

He gave the slightest smile. "Did you not hear? That the Son of Man was destined to suffer—but in three days to rise again?"

The full wonder of it suddenly broke through my shock and astonishment. He was the Lord, the Christ—and he had risen out of death! He was alive! I fell to my knees at his feet, speechless. I had to worship him. The risen Lord. I tried to touch, to hold his feet, but he backed away a little.

"Do not cling to me," he spoke gently. "Because I have not yet ascended to the Father."

"But my Lord," I murmured. "This is so wonderful. You are alive!"

"Mary," he spoke with even but authoritative tones. "There is one thing you must do for me. Go and find the brothers and tell them: I am ascending to my Father and your Father, to my God and your God. Tell them what you have seen. Tell them they must wait for me in Galilee."

I was reluctant to contemplate leaving him but could not disobey. And I certainly wanted to spread the news of what had come about.

"I will go, Lord," I said, still on my knees. "But my heart wants to stay with you for ever. How can I leave you?"

"There is work to be done," Jesus said. "And I need your help. Come." And he offered his hand to lift me up.

As I rose to my feet, we shared a look so wonderful, so deep, so full of love and mystery, that I thought I could never contain the joy that grew within me.

"Your heart will always live within my heart, Mary," he said.

"And I will love you always."

"Now go," he commanded.

For a few seconds I lingered there in the garden, lit with sunshine, birdsong filling the air. It was an entirely appropriate setting now. My soul sang with joy. And then I took to my heels and set off on the pathway back to spread the miraculous news to all the disciples, the women and everyone. I gave one backward glance, from some distance away, to try to catch a last glimpse of him, but he was nowhere to be seen.

Reflection

This mystery proves to be one of extraordinary change, from darkness to sunlight; from gloom to rejoicing; from death to inexplicable new life. Mary's despair is turned to hope, and her desire to sit grieving in silence with her dead Lord into a readiness to run rejoicing through a garden filled with birdsong in the service of her new-found Jesus. Amazing enough. Yet this mystery encompasses far more than a change of mood and the miraculous returning to life of a dead man.

Though Mary cannot comprehend it at the time, this event is testimony of the destruction of death's powers. Jesus has risen from the grave. It is God's defeat of the intentions of Satan to lead humankind into his own dark kingdom. It is the triumph of goodness over evil; the victory of God over all the lure and danger and consequences of sin. It is the transformation of the Cross from a shameful instrument of torture and death into the altar of sacrifice of the Lamb of God and the throne of God's mighty and merciful love.

Prayer

We praise you and thank you, Father in heaven, for the victory of the cross. We praise you and thank you for sending us your Son to give his life for us. We praise and thank you for breaking open the prison of death and saving us from the grip of sin. We pray for all the people today who still believe that death is the end and brings only oblivion. May they come to share an understanding of your mighty plan for humankind, and a love of the Saviour who destroyed death's hold and brought new hope into our world. We praise and thank you, eternal Father, because your Son was not held in the tomb, but burst out of the grave and showed his followers he was alive. We praise and thank you, God our Father, for our living Lord, Christ Jesus. Amen

2. The Ascension

The Ascension of our Lord to heaven, the second Glorious Mystery, represents the very moment of Christ's leaving this world at the end of his ministry and his returning to his Father. We can only imagine the welcome he must have received! For a long time before this, Jesus had been preparing his disciples— not only while he was with them before his death, but in the forty days immediately following, when, raised miraculously out of death, he repeatedly visited them in different groupings and in different locations. This story approaches the moment of the Ascension through this journey of preparation with one of these apostles, the one destined to become the chief shepherd of the flock, the rock on whom God would found His church.

Forty Days

Many looked back on those days as a time of wonder. Their grief turned readily to joy at such miraculous appearances from beyond the grave. But for me, this was the worst time of my whole life. Forty days of darkness. And I brought it on myself.

We were long ago accustomed to hardship, my brother and me. The lives of fishermen were never secure. Illness brought a family to hunger. A bad night at sea, a broken mast, a slip of a hammer in the boatyard—we had lived through poverty and pain. Bodily suffering I could have borne. But this was deep inside. Invisible. No one knew but I. Just as much as Judas, I had betrayed him.

"You were one of his followers, weren't you? Didn't I see you with him?"

The girl had caught me unawares. I didn't even think. I was alone among a crowd of them.

"No. No, not I." It was instinctive self-defence. I was in no state to get into an argument. My head was in a spin with the confusion of it all. Was this the end? Why had he not resisted arrest? Had it all been for nothing?

I was hidden in the crowd. The warmth of the glowing charcoal in the fire gave some primitive comfort, which I clung to like a sick child to its mother. But I glanced around. It was my undoing. A thin man, weasel-faced, eyed me keenly. "You're one of them."

"Never," I declared, drawing on what little strength I could muster. "You're mistaken, my friend."

He continued to stare at me suspiciously, but then another spoke to him, and his eyes turned away. I drew back a little from the firelight. Warmth had to be sacrificed for anonymity. But I came face to face with a big woman I had glimpsed earlier in the square.

"Hey, didn't I see you with this—Jesus?" She spat the word. "Before, in the crowd outside? It was you!"

For a second, I was speechless. It was her use of his name. In some dim way it began to open me up to what I was saying. But I was caught now in my lie. I could not change. The whole crowd was getting hostile.

"No. I wasn't there. It was someone else," I stuttered.

She grumbled her disbelief. There were other mutterings in the crowd. I was wishing I had a way to hide my face until some distraction shifted their interest and enabled me to slide inconspicuously away. I did not have long to wait.

A raucous cry sounded nearby. The rasping call of a cockerel at this inappropriate hour. All heads turned in amazement, but mine. The words of Jesus, our Lord, friend and leader for so long, came back to me. They rang like bells.

"Before the cock crows, Peter," he had said, "three times you will deny me."

I pulled back from the crowd and looked into the room. At the far end, they were taking him away out of the High Priest's house. I glimpsed him, one last time, and he seemed to direct his gaze at me. For a split second we shared a look. He neither smiled nor frowned. But his gaze went through my heart like flame. He had always known.

As he turned to go, I, too, twisted away. I could not watch him. Could not walk the same ground. Who was I? I had pledged so passionately that I would be with him, stay with him, come what may. I had meant it. Truly, I had meant it. But I had done the direct opposite. I was the worst of sinful men.

Turncoat. Hypocrite. It was worse than weakness. It was treachery. Towards the one who was the Lord of life, of healing, of miracles, of truth. He changed everything. How could I have disowned him? These thoughts flashed through me in seconds, and they were unbearable. All I could cope with was oblivion. I turned tail and fled.

I heard later of the way they treated our Lord. All the pain he went through, the scourging, the mockery, the piercing with nails, the long agony of crucifixion. My betrayal made it worse. I had become a part of those who ranged against him. It was anguish just to think it. Yet I could think of nothing else, again and again. They circled in my pulsing brain: the words I had said to those three people in the crowd; the words that Jesus had said of me.

They sought me out on the second day, the apostles. My silence and my desperation did not seem unusual to them. We were all lost, in our different ways. Until, on the third day, the women came with their weird tale of the tombstone being rolled away, of Jesus having disappeared.

"Come," said John. "We have to see."

He dragged me by the hand. I stumbled along with him, reluctant even to visit the grave of the Lord I had so basely betrayed. But at length I ran. The sheer exertion was relief of a kind. I ran past John at the entrance of the tomb, not stopping till I was right inside. There were white grave cloths on the ground, a faint smell of spices. Nothing else. John came and stood silently beside me. I could not believe what I was seeing. But John turned round to me with eyes wide with sudden understanding.

"In three days, I will rise again," he quoted. "Don't you see?"

I recalled these puzzling words again. Was this what it had meant? Had he risen somehow out of death? Then where was he? What did it mean for me, the one who had denied even knowing him? John must have read the fears in my face. He came over and embraced me. I felt suddenly exhausted, like a child.

I wept more tears in the next days. I wanted only to empty myself of everything. I heard the stories others told. It all seemed like a dream. The women said they had seen our Lord near the tomb. He had risen; he was alive! They told us he had asked us all to wait for him in Galilee. Two of the other disciples met him on the road to Emmaus. Amazed relief began to spread among them. And then he appeared to all of us, gathered in a closed room. While I tensed and cowered in shame, Thomas was brave enough to voice his doubts. Was Jesus just a ghost? Our Lord invited Thomas to feel his wounds, and Thomas fell to his knees. I wished I were able to do the same. But it was not for me, this joy they shared.

I went my own way. After many days I went back to the fishing boats. Perhaps it was best for me to get back to the old life. One night, a few of them came with me. We fished all night and caught nothing. As dawn broke, a man on the shore saw us approaching and called out to ask if we had a catch. When we had shouted back that we had not, he gave us instructions:

"Cast the net out on the right-hand side. You'll find something."

I thought he had a nerve, a stranger, directing seasoned fishermen, but the others were already releasing the net, so we let it fully out. When we came to haul it back in, it was so heavy with fish, it threatened to split and tear. I turned to look towards the man on the beach. My hands trembled. My heart felt the same flash of searing fire as when he had looked at me as he was leaving the house of Caiaphas. At the same instant, John spoke:

"It is the Lord."

There was no escape for me. Before I knew it, we were dragging the nets up the beach, closer and closer to the stranger who had called to us. He had bread and a charcoal fire waiting to roast some of the fish. The memory of that other charcoal fire jolted sickeningly from the shadows of my mind. Did he mean to make a point?

"Bring some here," he said. "We'll have a breakfast."

I obeyed. When the fish was cooked, he broke the bread and gave it to us, followed by the fish. We ate, almost in silence. No one dared to ask, yet all of us knew. He was Jesus, the Christ. But there was something subtly different about him: a smoothness in his movements, less robustness in the bone, a peaceful gravity. How it made me long to share in his life again! If only for a moment— to know his gentle love. But I sat a little apart and ate my meal in silence.

A shadow fell across me just as I was finishing. I looked up. Jesus had come across the shingle, and now lowered himself to kneel before me. I could not look into his face.

"Peter," he asked me softly. "Do you love me more than these?"

Love? I was astonished. Did he still think me worthy of loving him, the risen Lord of heaven and Earth? To love him was everything I had lost and everything I wanted. My heart was leaping like a crazy dog.

"Yes, Lord," I gasped. "You know I love you."

"Feed my lambs."

I was wondering at this, and still not daring to look up, when he said again:

"Simon Peter, do you love me?"

"Yes, Lord," I answered, beginning to ask myself why he should ask the same question twice. "You know I love you."

"Look after my sheep."

I hardly dared to word the thought that crossed my mind. Was he asking me to serve again, as a shepherd of his people? When other disciples were far worthier than I? I was about to look up, when his voice repeated:

"Peter, do you love me?"

Three times. Three times he asked me to declare my love for him – because three times I had denied him. There were tears, springing helpless from my eyes, when I looked up into his face. His eyes were dark, loving, and serious. He held my gaze a long time. I knew this moment mattered. He was breaking down the darkness I had put between us.

"Yes, Lord," I replied at last. "You know everything. You know that I love you."

"Feed my sheep," he repeated.

The welling up of both gratitude and tears prevented my assenting aloud, but he knew. He understood. He rose to his feet and, with arms outstretched, welcomed me into his embrace. I mumbled my huge thanks as I, for some moments, wrapped my arms round him. He felt as physically real to me as he had been before to Thomas. It was a breath-taking moment. I thought it marked the end of all those weeks of dread. A new and profound joy sparked within me and flared through every part of my being. Jesus, my Lord, trusted me again! I knew now that I must change for ever. Silently I vowed to be faithful every moment to my calling. I was his. I was the shepherd of his sheep.

Jesus released me from his embrace, but held my wrists now in his hands, close together between us, as if to be sure of my attention. He was saying something else.

"When you were young," he observed, "you could put on your own belt and do as you pleased; but when you grow old, someone else will put a belt round you and take you where you would rather not go."

I heard the words, and the sober tone —the warning that it would not be easy. A sudden hollowness opened up inside me. There would be huge challenges. Did he already know that I would fail? Or could I really be faithful through new and daunting trials? I had betrayed him once. Would I fail again? It threw a chill into the warmth of my newfound joy, but Jesus seemed not to notice.

"Follow me," he said.

I nodded, struck dumb now, as he turned with his new fluid movements and crossed the beach to join the other disciples. I gathered myself together and trailed across behind him. He was addressing all of them, but I was lost in thought.

Several days later, he came to us again in Bethany. He talked to us for a long time at table on the subject of the scriptures. He opened new understanding for us; it was amazing. I was enthralled. He was so sure; so convincingly authoritative. I wished I could be like him. I desired so much to serve him with utter faithfulness. And yet, in my mind that doubt lingered. When we walked, a little later, out onto the hillside in the outskirts of Bethany, I was still torn. I think he knew what troubled me. He came and walked beside me.

"I am soon to return to my Father," Jesus explained as we walked. "You must stay in Jerusalem. Wait for what the Father has promised."

There was a rustle of hushed conversation among my fellow disciples. He knew they were wondering what this meant.

"It will be," he said, more loudly, "what you have heard me speak about. John baptised with water, but you, not many days from now, will be baptised with the Holy Spirit."

He looked round at us all, but as he went on, his gaze settled quite fixedly on me.

"I will send you what the Father has promised. Wait in the city then, until you are clothed with the power from on high."

Something within me began to stir with new excitement. What was this power from on high? A deeper faith? Courage? The strength to follow him without doubts or wavering?

Thomas and James began to ask when this would happen.

"It is not for you to know the times and dates," he replied, "but you will receive power when the Holy Spirit comes on you, and then you will be my witnesses, not only in Jerusalem, but throughout Judaea and Samaria, and indeed to the ends of the Earth."

"Yes, Lord!" I broke out, filled afresh with enthusiasm. "We will tell your story. We will tell it to the world."

"In time," he murmured, stepping up onto a little mound beside the pathway, as if he planned to turn and address us all, as he often did in these quiet places. But he spoke no more. Something utterly amazing happened instead. It came about before our very eyes, yet it is hard to remember just exactly what occurred.

It was as if a cloud gathered. There was misty vapour round his feet at first, but it thickened rapidly until it seemed to lift him from the ground. I lost sight of everything around me at that point. I was just aware of Jesus in the cloud and a blue space like sky all round him, very bright. He rose into this blue sky, quite rapidly in the end, until he was whisked away into the heavens above our heads. I think we were all gazing skyward, unaware of one another, lost from the real world because it shocked us all when a voice close by spoke out.

"Why are you men from Galilee standing here looking into the sky?"

I turned to see two men, dressed in white garments, golden-haired, standing on the pathway.

"Jesus, who has been taken up from you into heaven," said one, gazing at us from startling blue eyes, "this same Jesus will come back in the same way as you have seen him go there."

I gazed at the two majestic figures. There was a beauty in them both. I thought they had to be angels.

"Will he?" I asked.

"But he is gone from us now," remarked John.

It was said with a voice of sorrow. I could understand John's thoughts. We had lost our Saviour. He had so wonderfully, so amazingly returned to us from the dead, but now had left us. I moved across and placed a hand on John's shoulder.

"We must wait in Jerusalem," I said. "For the promise. Isn't that right?" I added, turning back to the angels for confirmation.

But they had vanished from sight. "We're on our own," said Andrew.

I wanted to say—yes, we are; but wait for the power from on high. Somehow, I knew we would find it a transforming experience. My heart was already beating in a new way. That chilling fear of failure had gone from me. There was eager anticipation in my heart instead. And there was love. Love of my Lord, Jesus Christ; and love of all these men who followed him and felt newly abandoned.

"Let's go home," I finally advised. "Tomorrow we must leave for Jerusalem, to be ready. To pray. The promise will be fulfilled."

Reflection

Peter, who has always lurched from hot to cold, from enthusiasm to humiliation, must have had the most turbulent of preparations for the Ascension of his Lord. Travelling in this story from the anguished guilt of betrayal to the joy of reconciliation, he is still not absolutely steadfast in confidence that he can obey the Lord's call. So, the final promise of Jesus just before he leaves the Earth, the promise of "power from on high", answers his pressing need. As this story ends, Peter's heart is open, ready to receive.

The ascent of Jesus into heaven is a source of almost unimaginable promises to us as well. As he rose, Jesus was still fully human and fully divine. He took our human nature, for the very first time, through the veil which had ripped open at his crucifixion, into the eternal kingdom of heaven. His Ascension created the doorway through which we can follow him into everlasting life. We, who were made in God's image, may come to look upon God Himself in heaven. We, too, need to be ready to receive.

Prayer

Jesus, we thank you because you came to Earth to be with us and rose from the dead to open up to us the road to heaven so that we may always be with you. God our Almighty Father, we praise you for glorifying your Son in this way—and for the astounding promise that we may come to share in his glory. Not because we are in any way worthy, but because of your love, your forgiveness and your gift of divine grace. May we, like Peter, be open to receive this wondrous gift. May we avoid the dangers of being too attached to the things of this life, and dream instead of the joys of the life to come. O faithful, loving and merciful God, keep us trusting and faithful always. Amen

3. The Descent of The Holy Spirit

The disciples had been told to wait in Jerusalem for "the power from on high". Then, Jesus had assured them, they would become his witnesses. Obediently, together with his mother Mary, they gathered in an upper room in the city to await whatever their master's words portended. Imagine their mixed feelings and their muddled ideas about what to expect. Yet they did not wait chattering about what this all meant. They were united in prayer for some considerable time. After Jesus' crucifixion, they had been divided, scattered in different directions, driven by fear of the future. Now, after his ascension, they act as one, unified by hope of a promise of something entirely new. In this hope they certainly were not disappointed. One of them, in this story, gives his own account.

A Letter from Jerusalem

From James, with his brother John, disciples of Jesus Christ in Jerusalem, to Zebedee, their father, with his wife, their mother, in Galilee, bringing greetings and amazing news!

Father, this letter must come as a shock. It's a surprise to me too. You well know I was never one for letter-writing. But something extraordinary has happened. I mean truly beyond and above the ordinary—not anything you'd ever even dream of. But definitely the kind of thing you just have to tell everyone about! I was already eager, desperate in fact, to tell the world, including you, my family at home, when the chance fell suddenly into my hands.

A fabric merchant from the north is here in Jerusalem, but he is to depart for home in a day or two and will be travelling close by Capernaum. He chanced to speak to me, to question me about what was happening because it's being talked about all over the town down here! When he heard where I was from originally, he offered to take a letter for me. So here I am sitting down and writing. Wonder of wonders, you must be thinking. James, with a pen in his hand! I've changed from the days of handling those heavy tools in the boatyard, and the heavy nets on board ship! We catch a different kind of fish, these days.

This makes me remember how hard it must have been for both of you, when John and I had to leave as abruptly as we did. It was a call we couldn't refuse, and I think when I've told you this tale you'll understand. But I'm sorry it had to be so hard for you. And I hope young Nathan's big enough by now to manage the nets. I'm sure he's a fine young fellow and a support to you both.

It's a good while now since we were all in Galilee, and you saw us with Jesus, the man who attracted us to be his disciples. I expect mother remembers once, later on, asking his favour on our behalf, and being taken aback by his response! A lot has happened since then. We'd all come to truly believe that Jesus was the Son of God—yes, the Messiah, the one who would save the whole people of Israel and establish a new kingdom. I know you doubted it at first, and perhaps still do, but we followed faithfully, and we really thought we had come to know him well.

You may have heard about what happened a few weeks ago. I'm not sure how far that disastrous news has spread. Jesus' life came to a sudden end. Well, not altogether sudden, I suppose. He had infuriated the authorities for a long time and they wanted to bring him down, but he was the Messiah! How could he be outwitted by the leaders of the synagogue? But they captured him in the end. Pontius Pilate tried him and handed him over to the people and the military for crucifixion. Jesus had even predicted his own death, though in strange words that we couldn't understand, or wouldn't understand, because we simply refused to believe it. When it actually happened, it was an earthquake for us. The world we knew was no more. We scattered; we panicked; we couldn't see a future.

Jesus had told us he would rise again on the third day. But what did that mean? We thought his words were madness, or at least incomprehensible. Yet from the third day after his death and burial, various reports reached us that Jesus had been seen again! Women visiting the tomb found it opened and the body of our Lord missing. He appeared to two disciples on the open road—and ate supper with them. And he appeared to all of us, inside the house, although the doors were closed. He was tranquil and different and wished us peace. And one day he instructed us to stay in the city until we were 'clothed with the power from on high'.

More strange words. But we knew better now than to doubt them. We stayed in the city. Even after he finally told us these appearances had to come to an end, as he had to return to his Father in heaven. Even after he allowed us to witness—to see with our own astonished eyes—his rising to heaven, his disappearance into clouds that raised him above the Earth into the skies. I know you may be shaking your heads, but I swear this is all true. Jesus died and is risen – and the most amazing part is still to come – what I really want to write to you about!

We still remained, waiting in the city after this, though not knowing exactly what we were waiting for. We gathered together often, and we prayed together for his guidance and wisdom. Sometimes the mother of Jesus was with us as well. That's how it was when Pentecost came round. We gathered in the upper room, where Jesus had celebrated Passover: Mary, we eleven old disciples, and Matthias our new brother, who joined us to replace Judas Iscariot, who played a heinous part in bringing Jesus down. We were just praying together in this big room. Praying together, but in a way each of us was separate. We were all clinging to hope, but each of us was challenged in a different way—heartbroken to lose his presence, disillusioned about there ever being a new kingdom, uncertain of the future. So much was churning in our hearts beneath the surface. But we kept a silence. There were sounds only of breathing, and occasional sighs. We settled, used to the quiet. Mary kept a perfect stillness—influencing all of us, I think.

Then in the briefest time imaginable everything changed. There was a deep, distant noise like thunder. It grew louder and closer. We were all distracted from prayer, shocked, looking around. The noise overwhelmed us, and a great wind began swirling in the room. I swear the building rocked in this great clamour. Grown men, we were, and we clutched at one another. It was no ordinary storm. I saw eyes roll in fear. I supported myself against one of the pillars and felt the fierce vibrations beneath my hand. The whole place shook. Would the roof fall?

I glanced up to check if there was damage to the vaulted ceiling of the room, and there it was. Well, it... I didn't know what it was. It came and went at first. A glow, a reddish light, a lick of flame. I swear I didn't breathe for ages. This flame lapped around the ceiling, curling round the pillars, as if it was alive.

I know you might be thinking we were drunk. We were accused of precisely that by the folk outside. But we were sober; we hadn't touched a drop. And then this fire began to crawl, like snakes, down all the pillars. We stared, open-mouthed. It made a leap towards us. It touched Peter first. I really thought his hair would all catch fire and blaze. So did we all. There was such a horrified gasp. Had things gone horribly wrong? Were we all going to perish in a furnace?

But Peter didn't burn and nor did I. This fire kind of jumped, from Peter to Andrew. Then to John and on to me. It didn't harm. It wasn't hot. It wasn't fire at all. It seemed to dance on all our heads as though it was having a game. I saw Mary smile. Andrew laughed out loud. Matthew was the first to get up and start to dance. For a few seconds it was like a party. Father, this is truth—believe me—it truly happened. We pointed at each other, with this fire on our heads. We laughed and we danced. I know you'll think I must be going mad. I guess it was a few moments' hysteria. We were hugging each other in a delirium of relief and friendship and joy.

Pretty soon we saw the flames grow fainter until at last they disappeared. It calmed us down. But such a glow flamed still within our hearts. We all felt it. It hadn't left us, this flaring vision, it had penetrated us. It flared within. We gazed at one another with new eyes filled with excitement and a new conviction. Father, I swear I've never felt anything like it before. It dawned gradually on all of us that this was what we had gathered for. It was what Jesus had planned. It was the Holy Spirit that he had promised. The power from on high. And it was wonderful. We gathered in a circle again and knelt down. No one said a word, but I knew everyone was giving thanks. It was so real. Jesus was so real—so present with us in a different kind of way. His love was palpable. I never wanted to leave.

Except of course, we knew we had to tell everyone. Just as I have this driving need to tell you. I want you to know and to understand. Jesus was and is still the true Son of God. Who else could have filled us with the fire of his very being? We all felt a real passion to spread our news. So, by ones and twos we went out into the crowds and talked to everyone passing by outside. And words came out of our mouths that we hadn't thought up ourselves.

Seriously. I mean sometimes words from a different language. You know how many languages you find in a city like Jerusalem. Well, everyone we spoke to heard us speaking in their own tongue. Rumours spread around the streets. More people came flocking. Including my merchant who is to take you this letter. And the more we told them of the truth of Jesus Christ, the more they were amazed at the words that came out of our mouths. They were all questioning one another as to how this could be. How could we speak all these languages when we were simple Galileans? And we were telling them it was the pure work of the Holy Spirit of Jesus Christ. Excitement flashed round the city until hundreds must have heard about what was going on.

Of course, in the end, a lot of them decided we were drunk. There was so much perplexity and gossip going round, mixed now with mockery and laughter, that the city was on the brink of riot and some of us were growing concerned for the women and children in the crowd. And then Peter amazed us.

Peter, the inconstant Peter, right one moment and wrong the next, certain one moment and devastated by his own failures at the next, dear volatile, vulnerable Peter—he stood up on a plinth in the midst of everyone and addressed the people in a voice of such calm authority, that they quieted and listened as he told them the story of Jesus. It was a new vision. It was our world now. I think we all knew it. This was our future. The doubts, the heartbreak, the disillusion had all vanished away—burnt in the fire of the coming of the Holy Spirit. We had the power now to be the witnesses who would spread the good news to all the world.

Father, I am changed. For the better. For something wonderful that still lies in the future. I will pray for you both that you might fully join me in sharing this faith. I pray that you will come to understand and to love our Saviour, Jesus Christ as much as I do.

I hope you will recognise that this letter, though unexpected, comes not from a drunken or demented individual, but from your own son James, with the most earnest love, inspired by a new infilling of the Holy Spirit of God. May it awaken you to new life. May he grant you both the blessings of his peace and love and wisdom. Amen. Amen.

Reflection

"Not many days from now you will be baptised with the Holy Spirit," Jesus had foretold. The disciples had no idea what this could mean. What a difference now! James reveals his excitement and new enthusiasm, and his letter home testifies to Peter's new-found confidence and wisdom. They are changed men. They have become the leaders of the new Church. They are filled with a new desire; they are irresistibly propelled into spreading their story far and wide. The seed of the Church has matured and come to birth. Because of the breakthrough which Jesus' Ascension has made between heaven and Earth, the Holy Spirit has been freed to come to human lives on Earth in a new and powerful way—in tongues of divine fire. The hearts of the disciples, kindled by that fire, are ablaze.

Baptism in the Holy Spirit was not intended only for the disciples. They passed it on, laid hands on others, Jews and Gentiles, in the ensuing weeks and years, so that they, too, would receive the Holy Spirit. This life-changing gift is still the same today. Though perhaps most of us were baptised in the Spirit as babies, we can receive a new baptism, a new infilling with God's holy fire, when we are older. It is a free gift of life in the fullness of God, for everyone who will ask.

Prayer

Holy Spirit, we praise you for your power, your wisdom and your love. We thank you, Spirit of truth, for coming into our world at Pentecost and for transforming the lives of the apostles. Help us to pray as steadfastly as they did. Help us to be open to you, ready to allow our lives to change. Come to us, breath of God. Live in us. Empower us to spread the Gospel story in today's desperately needy world. We are so weak on our own. Fill us with new life. Transform us, we pray, Holy Spirit, and enkindle your fire in our hearts. Amen

4. The Assumption of Mary

As we approach the ending of the Rosary, we move into more mysterious depths. These final Glorious Mysteries contain things which none of us have even remotely experienced. There is little guaranteed authentic written evidence about Mary's last years, but the Church in her wisdom is in no doubt that the body of Mary, who brought God to birth in her womb, would not have been allowed to experience earthly corruption. The Assumption is the mystery of her being taken, body and soul, directly up to heaven after her death (perhaps not quite so swiftly as in this story). Several artists have painted a scene where Mary, like a small child, is carried heavenward in her Son's arms. It is a beautiful reversal of the presentation of Jesus in the temple in his mother's arms so many years before. This story is offered as a humble attempt to imagine how it might have been.

Last Journey

She was sinking fast, this aged lady. Sadly diminished from the strong and striking figure she had been in her middle years, Mary lay now, mute and unmoving on a low cot in a small and simple room in a small house in the outskirts of Jerusalem.

Her cousins and friends tended to her few needs. She ate next to nothing, and she lay still all day and all night, except when they came to turn her, to protect her from sores. Gone were her active years, her amazing and miraculous years when she became the mother of the new Messiah. Gone was the suffering of his early and horrific death, and the joy of his wonderful rising out of that death. What a life she had led! But gone now, even, were the days when she could at least sit by the window and reflect on the world going by on the street outside. She was too weak to sit.

She spoke to them no more. Her breathing was almost imperceptible. They could not tell whether her heart was moved with feelings anymore, or whether her mind held thoughts. They imagined everything was fading away. Distant family members had been summoned. Her helpers moistened her lips, sat at her side, prayed in the long, enduring silence and waited.

As Mary had waited. Patient by nature, Mary was skilled in the art of waiting. As a child she had waited to know what God wanted her to do in her life. As a mother she had waited as her child grew slowly to maturity. At the foot of the cross, she had waited. And through all of it she had listened for the voice of God. Through all these last months, weeks and days, she listened also to her beloved son. He was always there, and inside her mind she spoke to him.

As her consciousness sank first from the outside sickroom realities into the memories that thronged her mind, she shared all their special moments with him. Do you remember, do you remember? She would nudge his recollections of his childhood days. She would remind him of the wedding where the wine had run short, and the first signs of his divinity had broken forth. My heart sang then, she told him. And it still sings now.

Weeks had passed since then, and the details of the memories slowly faded. Their edges blurred; their landscape misted over. But she knew they were still there. It was just that she no longer walked through their vivid outlines and colours. It was like being a misty cloud. She floated among them. And still her soul sang in thanksgiving.

Later still, the words of the song faded. It was a silent music now which flowed like water through her days. Her life, her memories had altered now, from sequences of things and places and events, into a continuity, a liquid flowing down long, shifting years. She was a river, it seemed to her. Yes, she was a watercourse, abruptly hollowed in parts by life's shocks or sufferings, smoother in other more tranquil stretches. And she was the water which had travelled from some unknown source, through gentle channels, over jagged, tumbling rocks and into steady, contemplative pools.

I am flowing somewhere, she said to Jesus. She did not know where. Nor did it concern her. She sensed a new kind of expanding freedom. It was filled with bliss. The most wonderful journey of all, she said to him. She was like the river still, she thought, only it was growing and widening. It was a river reaching the end of its course and flowing, oh so gently, into a broader sea. She was water sliding into undiscovered depths.

As time passed, she grew to feel lighter still. There were no more words. She was cloud, she was vapour, rising in the sky. She was mingled with her son in a much more elemental way than talking with him, or even holding him, touching face to face, like mother and child. He drifted with her now on this journey. Into light, it seemed to her. Into joy.

The seams of light ahead of her grew stronger. Like shafts of sunlight strengthening and opening up the clouds. A huge light beckoned, and she longed to reach it. Her son urged her on too. They seemed to fly now together, like birds towards the sun. She would fly, yes. She would fly with him to heaven. She let go. She shook off all the water of earthly memories, and lifted, like strong birds' wings, out of the hold of the world and headed for the sky.

Mary's cousin Sarah sensed the change. She rose to her feet and leaned over the low cot, trying to detect her patient's breathing. All seemed silent. She watched and listened intently as minutes passed. She began to think she could even detect Mary's complexion paling. She must be imagining things. She touched her cousin's hand, and then held it in her own. It had already grown cold.

Sarah's heart chilled too, echoing the change in Mary. And for a long time, she did not move. The chill hand, the closed eyes, the emptiness somehow did not disturb her. Nor did she feel any need to rush into action. It was the peace which emanated from her, she realised. She had died in peace. God had rewarded her surrendered life.

Before she left to spread the news, Sarah praised the Lord in tears.

In the new world of light, Mary had come to rest. The lengthy, flowing and flying movements of her life's journey had slowed and very gradually ceased. She was held still; like a bird suspended on the wing in steady air. But more restful; as if those river currents curled and settled now, becoming still water in a deep pool. She felt almost cradled. Yes, for it was warm and comfortable; it was like the reassurance of love. Her heart gave thanks. She allowed herself simply to rest in this new embrace of peace.

She never wanted it to end, but gradually she became aware of thoughts stirring in her own mind. Had it been a dream? Was she about to waken on her sickbed, to discover only darkness and the lamp which Sarah would have lighted as the night came on? She tried not to think. The sense of being loved here was palpable, and she wanted to stay, she wanted it to endure, even if in the end it proved illusory. She tried to sink into the bliss of simply resting once again. But something gently jolted her to a different level of awareness. Was it her son? Had Jesus truly travelled here with her? Was he still here? She tried to turn, to look around. There was a totally new sensation of motion in her; she almost gasped. But she could see nothing. The light was so strong it blinded her. Yet, very slowly, as she gazed into it, she began to see its clouds and movement, its rippling waves. And then within them, a darker shape began to form. She strained to see. A figure, was it? A head, a face? Hazily at first, she began to perceive him. A circle of darkness, like a frame around a paler centre, swam out of the light for a moment, but then a wave of glistening brightness washed across her vision and the image disappeared. Still, she gazed. And after a while the cloud of light shifted, faded, and she saw him again. The darkness was his hair, and in the face, still mistily unclear, were the dark shapes of his eyes.

"Do you see me?" he asked.

Still, she stared. Her focus seemed to come and go. And then he came nearer and emerged suddenly from the bright cloud. Her son. Her beloved son. As clear as day. She saw his face, his dark, loving eyes, a huge smile. She saw that his body was clothed in white, and that his arm reached towards her. Her hand felt the touch of his. She was shocked: startled by the depth of breaking joy.

"Jesus," she breathed.

"Welcome," he said, holding her hand in his. "Welcome to your eternal home."

"It's so good..." she stammered, too amazed to think properly. "So good... to see you... my lovely son."

"This is my Father's house," Jesus explained, giving a wide, expansive gesture with his free arm. "He bids you welcome here."

"You look so beautiful!" Mary gasped abruptly, for it was true. She could think of nothing else—he looked astonishing.

"And so do you."

"Oh no!" she gasped. "Not like you."

"Look," he said, lifting up her hand which lay in his. She stared, blinking, at her own hand. Gone were the hollows between the old bones of her hand, and gone the raised veins which had previously clambered over the bones like stems on a trellis. It was a young hand. She gazed in disbelief.

"My Father so delights in you," Jesus explained, leaning closer, "that he would not leave you to the earthly forces of ageing, of death, of decay."　．

Mary, shocked now into a full new consciousness, was struggling to rise. To her amazement, before she had even really begun the effort, she stood full height before him. Age had dropped from her. She stood firmly, like a girl.

"But…" she stammered again. "But…"

Jesus laughed, straightening up himself from the crouched position he had taken beside her. "I came to fetch you. My Father sent me to fetch you. Can you not hear the angels waiting to accompany us?"

"Angels?" She listened. There was a strange music in the air, faint, but growing stronger. "Yes," she said, tentatively.

"Look," he said. "Look around."

As she obeyed and looked about, gazing into the brightness of this new world, it did seem to her that something moved in the clouds about them. Waves of light, a sweeping movement in the misty air, a drifting gold. Gradually she began to see that it was the movement of wings. She drew breath audibly in awestruck surprise.

"They have come to welcome you, my dearest mother."

She was speechless, happy, incredulous. She moved towards him. He stood before her in a long, simple, sleeved white robe, tied with a slim rope around his waist. His face seemed to her unbelievably beautiful.

"I love you," she said. "I don't know what to say. Except thank you – thank you, my dear son. Thank you for your welcome here."

She raised her hands to his shoulders, and he wrapped his arms around her. For a while they held each other in a close embrace, and she felt the strange new mingling of their changed, unearthly bodies. It moved her, like intoxication. She had never known such happiness as this. The music of the angels swelled about them.

At last mother and son drew apart. "Come," said Jesus. Mary nodded her willingness.

So, taking his mother's hand, and surrounded by a cloud of angels with accompanying music, sweet as bells, he led her deeper into the Kingdom.

When Sarah returned to the little house on the Jerusalem side street, she brought other friends. They came to help in the washing and laying out of Mary's body, or simply to be there and to mourn the passing of their friend, the long-widowed, long-grieving, ageing mother of Jesus Christ. Sarah pushed open the door into the room. A huge gasp broke from her.

"What is it?" the friends questioned. "What's wrong?" Sarah shook her head and gave no answer.

All of them eventually filed into the room. They stood around the bed, gazing and exchanging glances. The sheets had been turned back and the pillow straightened. But the bed was empty.

Reflection

Mary has been such a humble, holy and dedicated servant of God—yet much more than a servant. She consented to bear God's own Son in her womb. She is the spouse of the Holy Spirit, who overshadowed her to bring Jesus to conception. She became the Mother of God and nourished and raised and cared for this Son throughout his life. Her love knew no bounds and gave her great strength and endurance. She prompted him in his ministry and stayed with him through his worst trials, standing at the cross on which he died to share his pain. She was called by him to be the mother of the disciple John, and thus of all disciples and followers of Christ. She led the disciples in prayer at Pentecost in the upper room. She richly deserved to be assumed into God's eternal kingdom and take her place as first among the saints.

Prayer

Dear God, our Father, help us to honour Mary as she so superabundantly deserves. You honoured her by allowing her Assumption into heaven. We can never come close to her in holiness, humility, selflessness and dedicated love. But grant that we may imitate her to the limited extent of which we, with your help, are capable. Guide us on the way to holiness and help us pray for all those who have lost the strength of their earlier years and are approaching death. Through the guidance and benefit of her motherly love and the power of your grace, make us worthy to receive the wonder of eternal life in heaven which you have promised to believers. Amen

5. The Coronation of Mary

Mary was so intimately connected with all the persons of the Trinity of God, as obedient servant and daughter of the Father, spouse of the Spirit and mother of the Son, that perhaps it is no huge surprise that she should be given a special status in heaven—and a special role. Was she prepared for this, we might wonder? We have, once again, little idea from written works as to exactly how this happened. No one who lived to tell the story for us ever saw this coronation of the Virgin Mary as the Queen of Heaven. But surely many in heaven must have done so. One of those most drawn to be there at the ceremony must surely have been her faithful husband, Joseph. What might he have witnessed?

Queen of Heaven

She came at last, my wife, my beloved Mary. She was led here by our son and accompanied by a crowd of angels weaving their web of light and soft melody overhead. Her beauty shone from her in a way she was quite unaware of. She was shy, like a child awed by her new surroundings, and the gladness that came on her face when she saw me was wonderful to see. We stood gazing at one another in silence for a long time, while Jesus stood aside and watched.

"Dear Joseph," she said, her lovely voice like music, "I have missed you so much."

"And I you," I answered. "What a joy to see you here!"

She looked me up and down—the younger features I had acquired here, the youthful posture. I was used to it by now, but she—she gazed in unfeigned surprise and admiration, and then, with a laugh, looked down at her own girlish frame. She held out her young, unwrinkled hands, palms down, and laughed again.

"We have changed, Joseph. I never thought..." She broke off, with a shake of her head.

"You are a beauty," I remarked. "May I still embrace you like a husband?"

In answer, she came up close and raised her sweet arms to me. I held her in mine. We swayed, intermingled, in the new delicious harmony of heavenly touch. She drew back at last, gasping.

"Everything is so changed! So new!" she exclaimed. "And so strange." As she said this, she looked round into the spaces beyond us, but I could tell from the narrowed eyes and the little frown on her face, that she could make out very little as yet.

"You will see more," I explained, "when you have had time to adjust. It's not really so misty. It's just a kind of protection for you against the full impact of the light. Your eyes will be able to see our surroundings soon enough. Will you stay with me a while until that happens?"

Mary looked surprised. "I have come to stay with you always, now, I hope. You are still my husband, are you not?"

"Always," I said, "though none of us belong to each other in quite the way we did on Earth. And I think our dear son is waiting to take you further into the heart of the Kingdom, to meet the Father face to face, and to hear what he has to say."

"The Father—himself?" She looked startled.

"I am to take you to him," Jesus said quietly. "But there is no need to hurry. You can linger here as long as you wish."

Mary turned her eyes to Jesus and then back to me.

"The Father," she repeated. "But I am nothing. You cannot mean he wants to see me?"

"He sees you anyway," Jesus said, with an easy smile, "wherever you are. But yes, he wishes to meet you very greatly. He has things to tell you which will surely be best said face to face." He saw her anxious look. "But you have no cause to worry. That's the last thing he wants. You need time to adjust to this new world. He understands. He knows you so well already. So, stay a while until all grows familiar; it will be less daunting then. But yes, in the end, I will take you to meet our heavenly Father."

"An honour I surely don't deserve," Mary murmured. "But I will come, of course."

My dear wife, this new and young-faced Mary had no idea of her own importance. Which was precisely why she had been so eminently suited to her role in life. With me for occasional support, she had conceived and carried, given birth to and raised the Son of God on Earth, for the salvation of all humankind. She had loved him all the way into manhood. And she had stood by him through all the trials and pain and hideous agonies of his last days on Earth. It was through acceptance of all that suffering that he had won a victory on the cross for all humanity. He could not have done it if Mary had not consented to bring him into the human world within her womb. And then she could say she was nothing!

I adored her all the more. After all she had gone through, she was still at heart the girl I had met and fallen in love with. She was humble, and she was so beautiful she melted my heart all over again.

"I love you still, Mary," I said to her. "You are the girl I first met—but more besides."

"I love you," she answered, taking my hand and moving to stand close before me. "I will always love you, Joseph. I only wish to remain your wife and to serve God in whatever way he chooses."

Jesus came closer, smiling. "I hope you choose to be my mother also," he said.

"Jesus, my dear, dear son," she exclaimed, turning to him. "Of course, I am your mother always."

"And mother of John?"

She looked up into his face, her thoughts visibly shifting, before she nodded her agreement. "Yes, of course."

"And of all the apostles?"

"All of them?" She smiled in her turn. "Well, that was how it turned out, I suppose. I loved them all—and I don't mind that continuing, if it could. But can I be a mother to them still from here? It's such a different world!"

"You can, and more. You will see!" said Jesus. "But I will leave you with Joseph for a while. I will return to fetch you, when you are ready. Joseph will take good care of you."

"I will," said I.

It was a blessed, private time for the two of us, reunited now —at least for a while. We talked and laughed and cried together over everything that had happened in our lives, and everything that she had witnessed since my death. I had seen much of it, of course, from my new and amazing heavenly viewpoint, but I was happy to pretend to ignorance. It was so wonderful to hear her voice, her thoughts, her loving wisdom. She looked young again, but she had a greatness of soul that had only come from the long years of loving through the worst of sorrow and pain. I treasured those days we had together. I showed her about this new world a little and tried to introduce her gently to the new behaviour here of space and time. And I learned to love her all over again, in a far deeper and yet a more open way. I knew she was no longer exclusively mine.

When our son returned, I believed she was ready. "Will you not come too, Joseph?" she asked as Jesus took her by the hand, to lead her away.

"Not yet," I said. "But perhaps I will follow, in a little while. This is your time, my dear Mary. Go in peace."

Jesus had not confided in me what he knew about his Father's plans for Mary. But I had my suspicions! I knew how wonderfully he had greeted me, on my arrival in the heavenly realms. Despite my failings and my many weaknesses, my eternal Father had summoned me to his throne room and there lavished his love and thanks upon me. Thanks for caring for his earth-born son, for teaching, loving and training him; and thanks for treasuring the gift he had given me, of Mary, the virgin-mother of his only son. His reception had lauded me way beyond my deserts or expectations and held me in a warmth of love I had never before experienced. And I knew that for Mary, the reward of the Father's love would be overwhelming. I rejoiced for her already.

The call came, quite a short time later. Not a messenger, or a verbal invitation as we might expect on earth. Heaven's ways were familiar to me now. I felt the Father's call in my heart. And a way, a level, straight, new road, was opened up before me, and before all who were called. The landscape here adapts itself to need. When privacy is best it gathers itself into rounded valleys, secret dells, resting places of quiet and security. When we are to travel somewhere the land shifts over to open up a pathway, broad and direct. Distance seems telescoped. The briefest journey brought me to the place.

I had expected a greeting ceremony, a thanksgiving, perhaps once again in the chamber of the royal thrones. Or perhaps somewhere bigger, like a wide public square and an overlooking balcony. How humanity still coloured my thinking. In reality, I found myself in a vast spread valley, like an open dish, crowded already with thousands of people. I rushed to join them, and to my surprise, they parted, opening up a corridor for me to advance down the gradual slope towards the centre of the gathering. I demurred for a while, thinking there must be some mistake. But people ushered me forward, showed me only smiling and encouraging faces; so, I advanced and found my way right to the front of the crowd.

To my amazement, there before this vast crowd, was the throne room of the Father—the thrones, the steps up to them, the hangings, the golden light. But the walls were no longer enclosing it as I had seen it before. It was a spacious platform before us all. And at its sides were ranks of seats for the greatest of all the saints whom Jesus had brought from Sheol, after the three days he spent in the tomb. And behind the thrones were the great archangels. I was about to fall to my knees in worship at the sight of this magnificence, but an angel came to me and took my hand and ushered me to one of the seats at the side of the glowing central space. I hesitated, but the angel was insistent. So, I stepped up to the side of the great platform and took my place among the warmly welcoming saints of heaven. My heart was pulsing; this I had not expected. I sat waiting, awed already, surrounded by a wash of the sound of chanted worship and praise, and the singing of the angels.

When God the Father came to His throne it changed everything. The chanting and singing was hushed, the atmosphere transformed. I think everyone felt the same glow in their heart as the whole space filled with a new light and a powerful sense of God's love. Nothing else existed for a while except the cloud of light, golden, beautiful light, in which the Almighty was clothed. It was impossible to see exactly where He came from or at what moment He actually took His throne. But in those moments, no one cared. For the light—that golden light—was not simply light at all, I realised. It was love, grace, divinity, the Holy Spirit. It was joy.

Gradually this amazing light concentrated at the throne of God, and after some time we began to perceive the mighty figure of our eternal Father. His clothing floated about Him like mist in a wind. Flashes of rainbow colours scattered from it across the whole scene from time to time. As He turned, sometimes, we began to catch glimpses of His face. Beneath the drifting sea of His hair, a broad forehead and strong brows. Beneath those His eyes, deeply-set, wide with love. A strong, straight nose; the mouth almost hidden in a shifting cascade of moustache and beard. Looking directly at God, our Father, made it impossible to see the rest of the surroundings. He was all; He was everything.

Something made me look away nonetheless, towards the foot of the stairs, and there I saw two figures approaching and mounting up the stairway—Jesus and Mary. I watched my approaching wife and son, stepping steadily into the glorious light of the Father's presence. Mary wore a long robe of gold, with a light, golden veil on her head. Jesus, tall, with a new grace I had not seen before, led her by the hand. He wore a white robe, glowing like silver, tied with red around his waist. My heart filled with such love for them both that I felt I could hardly contain it. I watched the ceremony rapt and silent.

They knelt before the throne of God and listened to His words. I think, in my excitement, I only really took in half of them. He greeted Mary warmly as His precious daughter. He told her how delighted He was to welcome her, and how beloved she was of all the people. I was told later how the people cheered, but I was scarcely conscious of it at the time. He greeted His Son also, and then said He wished to confer glory on His beloved Mary and asked her what was her desire. For a while she said nothing, and He prompted her again.

"I have no wish for anything, almighty Father," she said at last, "except just to live here in your joy and peace, to do your will, to spend time with my husband and my son."

"And if I said that my will is that you love and nurture all my people, and help to bring them all into my kingdom, what would you say?"

"That there is nothing I would rather do, Lord."

"You have no personal request?"

"No, my dear Father. What you have said is my request."

"Then it is granted."

I was so lost in admiration of her clear simplicity, which was no longer that of a child, but of a mature confidence, that it startled me to see that Jesus had stepped forward and was making a request of his own. I only caught his last words— but they were staggering: "...that she be crowned the Queen of Heaven."

"Be it so," came the mighty voice of God. "She shall be the Queen of Heaven, and she shall be the Blessed Mother of all my children on Earth. She will lead souls into my kingdom."

I could see that Mary looked up, large-eyed. She must have felt overwhelmed.

"Will you protect my people? Will you lead them to love your Son and my Son, Jesus Christ? Will you do this for me, Mary?"

"I will," answered Mary after the briefest pause. "Yes, I will."

While my head whirled, Jesus was already leading his mother to the throne which stood empty on the left of his Father's, and a procession of mighty angels with golden wings was approaching up the stairs. Mary took her seat on the magnificent throne, with a grace that took my breath, and when she had settled, facing all the people now, the newly arrived angels formed a semicircle round Jesus and his mother and worshipped on their knees. It seemed to me there was a new music in the skies. Our Father God watched benignly in His glory. One of the angels rose and lightly whisked away the golden veil that Mary had been wearing, and another presented a golden crown to the Son of God (I could not think of him as my son anymore). He took it between his hands, advanced a couple of paces to stand before his mother, lifted the crown high in the air and then slowly lowered it and gently positioned it on his mother's head. She looked amazingly calm; she looked magnificent.

Jesus stepped back, and then the wave of sound from all the people overwhelmed me.

"Queen of Heaven, Queen of Heaven!" they chanted.

As they did so, other angels brought her gifts: caskets of gold, strange treasures, jewels, necklaces, huge lily flowers—I could no longer see for tears of joy. She plainly did not know quite what to do with them, and in the end, she held only the glorious lilies, while the angels stood on either side holding the other gifts. Jesus had moved away and at his Father's prompting, took his seat on the throne at the Father's right-hand side.

In the swelling of praise and music which drew the ceremony to its close, God the Father rose majestically to His feet. The cloud of light around Him shimmered and intensified. All the people, angels, and all the saints—and I myself among them—fell to our knees, some prostrating themselves, in adoration and worship. Joyful song filled the air. The Father raised His arms, giving a glimpse of large, well-muscled limbs within His filmy clothing, and held them out at either side, an invitation to His beloved Son and the new Queen of Heaven, His honoured daughter and my transformed wife. Jesus rose to his feet, to loud acclaim, took his Father's hand and stood, tall and slender, close beside his Father and within the inner cloud of intense divine light. As Mary rose from her unaccustomed throne and turned towards the brightness of God, however, her eyes were downcast, and she hesitated momentarily before sinking, overwhelmed at confronting the blaze of his glory, onto her knees before Him. He held His hand over her crowned head and uttered words of benediction and thanksgiving.

Reflection

Joseph, who determined to marry Mary as a young girl, in spite of contrary worldly advice, now witnesses her extraordinary elevation as she becomes the Queen of Heaven. What a way she has travelled! No wonder Joseph is overwhelmed. What a way we have travelled with her, as she has led us all through these mysteries of her Holy Rosary. Now she is not only Queen of Heaven, but Queen of the Church and mother of us all. She is uniquely positioned with experience of humanity which gives her heavenly vantage point into our lives a special intimacy. She knows each one of us even more closely than our earthly mothers. She understands and speaks our language. Her position has even allowed her to visit us on earth in the places we now know as Marian shrines, which to this day keep their aura of our Mother's presence and an atmosphere of spiritual proximity to heaven.

We are exceptionally blessed in the gift God gave us in the Queenship of Mary. For she is of course as intimate with her risen Son, our Lord Jesus Christ, as she is with us. When we bring her our lives and our difficulties and ask her to pray for us, we can be assured her Son will listen. We should turn to her, consecrate our lives to her, and trust in her care, her guidance and her limitless love.

Prayer

Holy Mary, Mother of God and our beloved mother, you have led us through these mysteries along the pathway of your own life, from an unremarkable home in Nazareth to the heights of heaven and the glory of God. Permit us to stay close to you, to love you, imitate you and have recourse to you in every need. Bless us with your protection, your love and your intimacy with the Holy Spirit, so that we may never stray from faith in your divine Son, and, as he commanded, be filled with and driven by love for God and love for all humanity. We pray that

142

all our meditations and prayers on the Mysteries of your Holy Rosary might help to bring us more and more deeply into the fullness of life, the new creation, which your Son restored on earth. Amen

About the Author

Born in Huddersfield, Brenda gained an MA degree in English from London University. She married John and moved to Manchester where she taught English in various schools and FE colleges, and she and John had two children. As well as teaching, Brenda served as a Liberal Democrat councillor on Trafford MBC and maintained her writing hobby. After a vaguely Christian upbringing and the decision to be baptised and confirmed in the Anglican Church at the age of 15, Brenda had abandoned the faith at the time of starting university, believing it to be only wish-fulfilment. She remained agnostic for a great many years, until influenced by the faith of a committed Catholic colleague who led her to reconsideration and reception into the Catholic Church in 1990. Retired now from teaching, Brenda serves in a number of roles within the Church in Timperley, has organised pilgrimages and is a prayer group leader.